Better Homes and Gardens®

New JuNioR Cook Book

Houghton Mifflin Harcort

Boston New York

Library of Congress Cataloging-in-Publication Data is available upon request.

ISBN 978-1-118-14606-4 (cloth)

Printed in China.

SCP 10 9 8 7 6 5 4 3 2

4500462340

Meredith Corporation

Editorial Manager: Jan Miller

Editor: Sheena Chihak, RD

Contributing Editor: Marsha McCulloch, RD

Illustrator: Russell Benfanti

Photographer: Marty Baldwin

Recipe Development: Stephanie Karpinske, RD; Laura Marzen, RD; Nicole Peterson; Charles Worthington

Food Stylist: Sue Hoss, Main Dish Media

Publisher: Natalie Chapman

Associate Publisher: Jessica Goodman

Senior Editor: Linda Ingroia

Senior Editorial Assistant: Heather Dabah

Production Director: Diana Cisek

Production Editor: Abby Saul

Manufacturing Manager: Tom Hyland

Design Director: Ken Carlson, Waterbury Publications, Inc.

Associate Design Director: Doug Samuelson, Waterbury Publications, Inc.

Production Assistant: Mindy Samuelson, Waterbury Publications, Inc.

Our seal assures you that every recipe in *Better Homes and Gardens® New Junior Cook Book* has been tested in the Better Homes and Gardens® Test Kitchen. This means that each recipe is practical and reliable and meets our high standards of taste appeal. We guarantee your satisfaction with this book for as long as you own it.

CONTENTS

A NOTE TO PARENTS

Think back to the first recipe you ever made, the first time you stirred together ingredients in a bowl seemingly larger than you were, or the first time Mom let you crack an egg by yourself. Those little joys laid the foundation for kitchen competency. Introducing kids to cooking offers a time for creating memories while exposing them to practical life skills. Among many lessons, cooking teaches how to follow instructions, reading comprehension, time management, and pride in a job well done.

Involving kids in the kitchen also encourages healthful eating. Your child will appreciate a wider variety of ingredients and develop confidence to transform ingredients into delicious recipes. Have a picky eater? Helping to plan and prepare meals gives kids a sense of investment in the process so they are more likely to try new foods.

As a parent you know best the abilities of your little chef. It's your job to determine which steps children may safely complete alone and which require adult help. To avoid mishaps, talk to your kids to clarify and agree upon which tools and appliances are appropriate for them to use. Be certain they know what is off-limits and always be sure an adult is present when children are working in the kitchen.

Start with the basics, choose a recipe, and have fun! Encourage your kids to try something new and champion their culinary efforts.

Hey, kids! Grab an adult and head to the kitchen. It's time to get cooking! Turn the page to find everything you need to know to start your kitchen adventure. Learn how to read a recipe, measure ingredients, and identify cooking tools. With a little know-how, cooking is easy as pie!

BASICS

RECIPE FOR SUCCESS

Every recipe will turn out a winner if you follow these simple kitchen rules.

BEFORE YOU BEGIN

- Read the recipe from start to finish. Make sure you understand exactly what to do. If you don't, ask an adult for help.
- Check your ingredients. Be sure you have enough of all the required ingredients. If you don't, make a list of what you need and ask an adult to help you purchase them.
- If you have any food allergies, read the ingredients carefully to be sure all the foods are safe for you to eat.
- Gather all the tools you'll need to make the recipe.
- Wash up. Always wash your hands with soap and water for at least 20 seconds before you start cooking.

WHILE YOU'RE COOKING

- Measure ingredients accurately (see "Measure It Right," on page 7).
- Follow the recipe step-by-step. Finish each step in the recipe before starting the next.
- Use good food-safety habits (see "Kitchen Safety" on page 11).
- Always have an adult helper in the kitchen with you.

WHEN YOU'RE DONE

- Put leftovers away as soon as possible. Leftovers should never sit out for more than 2 hours.
- Clean up. Put away all ingredients and tools and throw away trash such as food wrappers. Load dirty dishes in the dishwasher or wash and dry them. Wipe counters with hot, soapy water. Wipe the table clean.

MEASURE IT RIGHT

The ingredient list is a simple formula that if you follow it correctly, will give you something delicious to eat. If you make a mistake measuring ingredients, you could end up with a disaster. Use these tips to master measuring!

MEASURING LIQUIDS

To measure liquid ingredients, use liquid measuring cups.* These are made of glass or clear plastic with a spout on the top. Liquid measuring cups have lines marked on them to show amounts.

To start, set the measuring cup on a flat surface. Pour in some of the liquid. Bend down so your eyes are level with the amount marks and see if you need more or less liquid.

Add or subtract little by little until you get to the right amount.

*Tip: For small amounts of liquid ingredients, such as vanilla, use measuring spoons instead of measuring cups.

MEASURING DRY INGREDIENTS

To measure dry ingredients, use metal or plastic measuring cups. These come in sets, each cup sized and marked for a different amount.

Spoon ingredients such as flour, sugar, nuts, and shredded cheese into the cup size called for.

Slide a metal spatula or knife across the top to make ingredients level with the top of the cup. Measuring spoons for smaller amounts of ingredients work the same way.

MEASURING SPECIAL INGREDIENTS

Brown sugar: Brown sugar needs to be measured differently than other sugars because it clumps. Spoon brown sugar into a dry measuring cup and use the back of a spoon to pack it firmly into the cup; add more as needed until it is level with the top of the cup. If done correctly, when you dump out the brown sugar, it will hold the shape of the cup.

Sticks of butter or margarine: One stick equals ½ cup. For smaller amounts, look for measurement marks on the wrapper and use a table knife to cut the wrapped stick at the mark you need. Unwrap the part you will use.

Shortening and peanut butter: First spray a dry measuring cup with nonstick cooking spray so food doesn't stick. Use a rubber scraper to pack shortening or peanut butter into the cup, making sure it's completely full. When the cup is full, level off the top with the flat edge of the rubber scraper. Use the rubber scraper to remove shortening or peanut butter from the cup. Be sure to scrape everything out.

MEASURING TIP
Never measure ingredients over the bowl or pan you'll put ingredients in. To avoid overfilling accidents, use a separate bowl to measure over.

KNOW THE TOOLS

Use this handy list to make sure you have the right tool for the job!

Sharp Knife

Cutting Board

Colanders

Saucepans

Electric Mixer

Table Knife

Pancake Turner

Wooden Spoon

Skillet

Kitchen Shears

Liquid
Measuring Cup

Dry
Measuring
Cups

Wire Cooling
Rack

Vegetable
Peeler

Wire Whisk

Tongs

Metal
Spatula

Muffin
Pan

Slotted
Spoon

Fine-Mesh
Sieve

Baking Sheet or
Cookie Sheet

Measuring
Spoons

KNOW THE LINGO

Use this list of cooking terms to help you make sense of any recipe you read.

Bake: Cook food in the oven.

Beat: Add air to a mixture and make it smooth. To beat by hand, mix the food with a fork or wooden spoon in a fast up-and-down motion, or use an electric mixer.

Boil: Cook food on top of the stove over high heat until lots of big bubbles form quickly and break on the surface.

Brown: Cook food until it starts to look brown on the outside. You can do this on the stove in a pan or in the oven with food such as cookies.

Chill: Refrigerate to make food completely cold.

Chop: Use a sharp knife—with an adult's help—and a cutting board. First slice food evenly, then cut slices into lots of small pieces about the size of a pea. Foods can also be chopped with a blender or food processor.

Combine: Mix ingredients together.

Cool: Let food stand on the counter until no longer hot. Putting food on a wire cooling rack will make it cool even more quickly.

Cover: Put plastic wrap, foil, or waxed paper over food to keep air out.

Dissolve: Stir a dry ingredient (like sugar) into a liquid (like water) until it disappears.

Drain: Put food in a colander to get rid of liquid and keep the solids.

Grate: Run an ingredient over the holes of a grater to break the ingredient into small pieces.

Grease: Spray a pan with nonstick cooking spray. You can also put some shortening or butter on a small piece of paper towel and rub evenly on the inside of a pan.

Melt: Heat a solid until it becomes liquid.

Mix: Stir ingredients together until a mixture looks the same all over.

Peel: Remove skin from vegetables or fruits with a vegetable peeler (as with carrots and potatoes) or your hands (as with bananas).

Shred: Rub an ingredient across a grater to make long, thin strips.

Simmer: Cook food on the stove over high heat until lots of small bubbles rise to the surface and break gently. Then turn the burner to low. Cover the food with a lid, if the recipe says to.

Slice: Use a sharp knife—with an adult's help—and a cutting board. Holding the food firmly on the board, cut a thin slice off the end. Repeat until all of the ingredient is cut into pieces of about the same thickness.

KITCHEN SAFETY

Great cooks are safe cooks. Avoid kitchen accidents with these safety tips:

HAVE AN ADULT HELPER

Have your adult helper read through the recipe with you to answer questions and show you how to properly use all equipment safely. Never use any equipment without permission. Always have an adult with you in the kitchen to supervise.

HANDLE THE HOT STUFF

Remember, anything you take from the oven, microwave, or stove will be hot! Use caution or ask your adult helper for help. Protect your hands with hot pads or oven mitts.

DON'T GET STEAMED

Tip lids open on saucepans and casserole dishes from the side farthest from you. This will let steam escape away from you, not at you.

TURN IT OFF

Before you scrape food out of a blender or food processor, turn off and unplug anything that was plugged into the wall. Always turn off the oven and stove top as soon as you're finished too.

KEEP APPLIANCES AWAY FROM WATER

Electric appliances (such as electric mixers) should never touch water. If an appliance falls into water while it's plugged in, DON'T TOUCH IT! Call an adult for help. Never plug in or unplug appliances when your hands are wet.

HANDLE WITH CARE

Always pick up sharp items such as knives by the handle. Don't forget to ask an adult for help and permission to use sharp tools.

KEEP FOOD SAFE

If food is not handled properly it could make you sick. Keep food safe using these rules:

- Only eat fresh foods. If it smells funny or is past the expiration date, throw it out.
- Wash all fruits and veggies in cool water before using.
- Avoid cross-contamination with a clean cutting board. Wash cutting boards immediately after use with raw poultry, meat, or fish and before using with any other foods. Always wash your hands after handling raw meat, poultry, or fish.
- Don't use cracked or dirty eggs. Always wash your hands after handling eggs.
- Never eat raw meat or eggs. These foods must be cooked to kill harmful bacteria.
- Check the temp. Cooked meats should be checked with an instant-read thermometer for doneness. Cook ground beef mixtures to 160°F, ground poultry mixtures to 165°F, and chicken breast halves to 170°F. Remember to store and chill leftovers as soon as possible. Don't let leftovers sit out for more than 2 hours.
- Keep cold foods cold. Foods stored in the refrigerator should be cold when you touch them. Frozen foods should be icy and firm. Don't thaw frozen foods on the counter; instead, thaw them in the refrigerator overnight so they stay cold.

STEP UP TO THE PLATE

To be healthy and full of energy, use MyPlate as an eating guide. It shows the five food groups you should choose from. To find the amount of each food group that is right for you, log on to choosemyplate.gov and click "Interactive Tools."

WHAT MAKES A GREAT PLATE?

Vegetables and Fruits: Fill half your plate with these. Red, orange, and dark green vegetables are especially good for you, so eat them every day. Add colorful fruits to salads, smoothies, cereal, and sandwiches.

Grains: The healthiest type is whole grains, such as brown rice, oatmeal, and whole wheat pasta. Popcorn counts too!

Protein: Choose different protein foods every day, such as lean meats, chicken, eggs, beans, nuts, seeds, and peanut butter. Eat fish twice a week. It helps keep your brain and heart healthy.

Dairy: Fit milk or yogurt on the side or enjoy cheese on top of other foods. Choose low-fat dairy products, such as skim or 1% milk.

WHAT'S IN A RECIPE?

The recipes in this book show how much of each food group you get per serving. Each symbol below represents one serving from that food group. At the end of each recipe you'll see symbols for the food groups in that recipe.

Vegetables =   Fruits =

Grains =   Protein =

Dairy =

GET IN THE GAME

Moving your body feels good and is fun. Exercise at least 60 minutes a day. Count all active times, such as recess, dance class, bike riding, and sports. Limit TV and computer time (except for homework) to 2 hours a day.

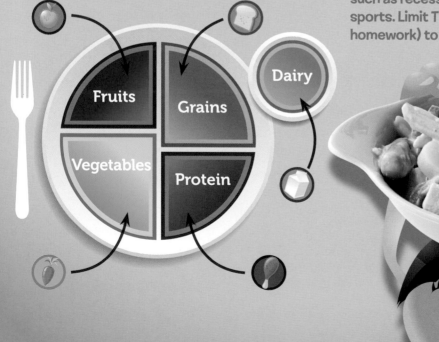

BE A LABEL DETECTIVE

Nutrition Facts labels and ingredient lists can help you make better choices. At the grocery store, help adults make good-health decisions:

NUTRIENTS TO LIMIT

Sugars: Compare labels on foods like cereal and granola bars to find ones with the least grams (g) of sugars.

Salt: Compare the milligrams (mg) of sodium in foods such as soups and breads and choose the foods with the lowest number.

Fat: Compare grams of fat in foods such as meat and ice cream to pick foods lowest in fat.

INGREDIENT CHECK

Few ingredients: Look for foods with short ingredient lists—they're generally better for you than packaged foods with long ingredient lists.

Whole grains: Choose bread, cereal, pasta, and crackers with the word "whole" as the first word in the ingredient list.

SWEET & SALTY TREATS

Some foods and drinks are OK to eat once in a while but not every day because they have lots of sugar, fat, and/or salt. Examples include cakes, candy, soda pop, pizza, chips, and fries. Pick one meal a week to eat such foods or have a sugary drink. Remember, water is the best everyday drink.

PARENT TO PARENT

You have more influence on what your kids eat than anyone else. Here's how to help:

- Fix food different ways. If kids turn up their noses at steamed asparagus, try broiling it. Kids can help brush spears lightly with oil and sprinkle them with grated Parmesan cheese.
- Eat meals together. The more often you do this, the better everyone will likely eat.
- Serve new foods with familiar ones. For example, offer sticks of fresh jicama sticks with a favorite low-fat dip. Ask kids to help shop for new foods too.
- Cut up raw vegetables and fruits. Everyone is more likely to dig in than if you leave them whole.
- Avoid offering sweets as rewards or to soothe disappointment. If you don't want kids to reach for ice cream when they've had a bad day, don't model this behavior.

POWER-UP BREAKFASTS

Time to refuel! Use these power-packed breakfasts to help you blast out of the house at lightning speed, gain super strength to haul a backpack to school, and give your energy a boost so you're ready for action.

BRAINIAC BLUEBERRY PARFAITS

Eating oats and berries helps keep you focused and sharp and makes you feel like you have superhuman smarts!

MAKES: 4 servings

Ingredients

- 4 cups regular rolled oats
- ⅓ cup shredded coconut
- ¼ cup sliced almonds
- ¼ cup dry-roasted unsalted sunflower kernels
- ¼ cup honey
- 3 tablespoons canola oil
- 2 tablespoons packed brown sugar
- ½ teaspoon ground cinnamon
- 1 cup plain or vanilla fat-free yogurt
- 2 tablespoons orange marmalade
- 1 cup fresh blueberries
- Fresh blueberries (optional)

Tools

Measuring cups, measuring spoons, medium bowl, spoons, 2 small bowls, 15x10x1-inch baking pan, wooden spoon, hot pads, baking sheet, foil or parchment paper, airtight storage container, four 10-ounce glasses

Let's Make It!

1 Turn on the oven to 350°F. To make granola,* put oats, coconut, almonds, and sunflower kernels in the medium bowl. Stir to mix well. Put honey, oil, brown sugar, and cinnamon in a small bowl. Stir to mix well. Drizzle honey mixture over oat mixture. Stir until oats are coated.

2 Pour oat-honey mixture into the baking pan. Spread into an even layer. Bake about 25 minutes or until light brown. Using the wooden spoon and hot pads, stir about every 10 minutes.

3 Line the baking sheet with foil or parchment paper. Use hot pads to remove granola from oven. Turn off oven. Spread granola out on prepared baking sheet. Set aside until cooled. Put granola into a storage container. Keep at room temperature for up to 1 week.

4 To make parfaits, put yogurt and marmalade in the other small bowl. Stir to mix well.

5 Put about 2 tablespoons of the blueberries in each of the glasses. Add about 2 tablespoons of the yogurt mixture to each glass. Add about 2 tablespoons of the granola to each glass. If you like, stir gently to mix. Repeat the same layers, but do not stir. If you like, top with a few more blueberries.

*Tip: If you don't have time to make the granola, substitute a healthful purchased granola.

PER PARFAIT: 201 cal., 6 g fat (1 g sat. fat), 1 mg chol., 59 mg sodium, 34 g carb., 3 g fiber, 7 g pro.

 X1

ELASTIC BOY EGG SANDWICHES

Stretch your energy all day by eating these easy egg-packed breakfast sandwiches!

Ingredients

Nonstick cooking spray

4 ounces cooked light chicken or turkey sausage, cut in half lengthwise and sliced

1 roma tomato, seeded and chopped

4 eggs, beaten

¼ cup shredded reduced-fat cheddar cheese (1 ounce)

4 whole grain English muffins, toasted, or whole grain bagel thins

Tools

Measuring cups, cutting board, sharp knife, medium bowl, wire whisk, shredder, toaster, medium nonstick skillet, silicone or wooden spatula, hot pads, spoon

18

Let's Make It!

1 Coat the skillet with cooking spray. Put on burner. Turn burner to medium-high heat. Add sausage to skillet. Cook about 4 minutes or just until sausage starts to brown. Stir all the time with the silicone or wooden spatula. Add tomato to skillet. Stir to mix.

2 Pour eggs into skillet. Cook over medium heat, without stirring, until mixture begins to set on bottom and around edges. With the spatula, lift and fold the partially cooked egg mixture so the uncooked portion flows underneath. Continue cooking for 2 to 3 minutes or until egg mixture is cooked through but is still glossy and moist. Sprinkle cheese on top of eggs. Use hot pads to remove skillet from heat. Turn off burner.

3 Spoon the eggs over muffin bottoms or bagel thins; add muffin tops.

PER SANDWICH: 291 cal., 12 g fat (4 g sat. fat), 237 mg chol., 702 mg sodium, 30 g carb., 5 g fiber, 18 g pro.

 X2   X2

MOVE IT!
Stretch your muscles every day to stay as flexible as Elastic Boy and to prevent injuries.

POWER SURGE BAKE

You'll bolt from bed for this sweet breakfast bake. Stuffed with fruit and cream cheese, it will electrify your morning.

Ingredients

Nonstick cooking spray

8 slices cinnamon-raisin bread

3 ounces reduced-fat cream cheese (Neufchâtel), softened

¼ cup strawberry or raspberry spreadable fruit

1 small apple, cored, halved, and thinly sliced

3 eggs

1 cup fat-free milk

¼ teaspoon salt

Powdered sugar

Tools

Measuring cups, measuring spoons, cutting board, sharp knife, 2-quart square baking dish, table knives, medium bowl, fork, wide spatula, foil, hot pads, wire cooling rack

Let's Make It!

1 Coat the baking dish with cooking spray. Set dish aside.

2 Spread 4 of the bread slices with the cream cheese. Spread the other 4 bread slices with the spreadable fruit. Arrange the apple slices on the bread that is spread with cream cheese. Top with the bread with spreadable fruit, spread sides down, to make sandwiches. Put the 4 sandwiches in the prepared baking dish.

3 Put eggs in the medium bowl and beat with the fork. Add milk and salt; beat until combined. Pour evenly over bread in baking dish. Use the back of the wide spatula to lightly press the bread down into the egg mixture. Cover with foil. Chill in the refrigerator for at least 2 hours or up to 24 hours.

4 Turn on the oven to 375°F. Bake for 25 minutes. Use hot pads to remove the foil. Bake for 10 to 15 minutes more or until the sandwiches puff up and you can't see the liquid anymore. Turn off oven. Use the hot pads to remove from oven and place on the wire rack. Let stand for 15 minutes.

5 Sprinkle with powdered sugar before serving.

PER SERVING: 349 cal., 11 g fat (4 g sat. fat), 156 mg chol., 515 mg sodium, 50 g carb., 2 g fiber, 12 g pro.

X½   X2   X½

21

ENERGY-BEAM BANANA PANCAKES

Transform pancakes into intergalactic space cakes by topping with fruit to look like flying saucers and adding banana meteors.

Ingredients

- ¾ cup whole wheat flour
- ¼ cup all-purpose flour
- 1 tablespoon sugar
- 1½ teaspoons baking powder
- ¼ teaspoon salt
- 2 medium bananas, peeled
- ⅓ cup maple syrup
- 1 egg
- 1 cup fat-free milk
- 1 teaspoon vanilla
- Shortening
- Orange slices and kiwifruit slices

Tools

Measuring cups, measuring spoons, cutting board, sharp knife, medium bowl, spoons, small saucepan, small bowl, fork, pastry brush, griddle or large skillet, pancake turner, baking sheet, hot pads, 6 dinner plates

Let's Make It!

1 Turn on the oven to 200°F. Put whole wheat flour, all-purpose flour, sugar, baking powder, and salt in the medium bowl. Stir to mix well. Set aside.

2 Slice 1 of the bananas. Put sliced banana and maple syrup in the small saucepan. Put saucepan on burner. Turn burner to low heat.

3 Put egg into the small bowl and beat with the fork. Use fork to mash the remaining banana. Add mashed banana, milk, and vanilla to egg. Beat with the fork until well mixed.

4 Add egg mixture to flour mixture. Stir until flour mixture is wet. The batter should be a little lumpy, not smooth.

5 Grease an unheated griddle or large skillet with shortening. Put on burner. Turn burner to medium heat and heat until a few drops of water sprinkled on the griddle or skillet dance across the surface.

6 For each pancake, pour about ⅓ cup of the batter onto the hot griddle. Cook 2 minutes or until surface is bubbly and edges are slightly dry. Use the pancake turner to turn the pancakes over. Cook about 2 minutes more or until bottoms are golden brown.

7 Transfer pancake to the baking sheet. Put into oven to keep warm. Repeat until all batter is used. Use more shortening to grease griddle or skillet, if needed. Turn off burner. Use hot pads to remove pancakes from oven. Turn off oven.

8 Place pancakes on plates. Arrange orange and kiwifruit slices on pancakes to look like flying saucers. Serve with warm banana-maple syrup mixture.

PER PANCAKE: 224 cal., 3 g fat (1 g sat. fat), 36 mg chol., 220 mg sodium, 45 g carb., 4 g fiber, 6 g pro.

X1   X½

23

EGG-TASTIC POWER PACKS

Charge your batteries with these industrial-strength breakfast bowls!

Ingredients

Nonstick cooking spray

4 slices whole wheat bread

5 eggs

1 tablespoon water

¼ teaspoon salt

1 teaspoon butter

¼ cup chunky salsa

½ cup shredded reduced-fat cheddar cheese (2 ounces)

¼ cup grape tomatoes, each cut in half

Tools

Measuring cups, measuring spoons, shredder, cutting board, sharp knife, muffin pan with four 2½-inch muffin cups, hot pads, small bowl, fork, medium nonstick skillet, silicone or wooden spatula

Let's Make It!

1 Turn on the oven to 350°F. To make toast cups, coat the muffin cups with cooking spray. Carefully press each bread slice into a muffin cup. Bake 8 to 10 minutes or until lightly browned and crisp. Turn off oven. Use hot pads to remove muffin pan from oven and set aside.

2 Put eggs into the small bowl and beat with the fork. Add the water and salt. Beat with fork until combined.

3 Put butter in the skillet. Put on burner. Turn burner to medium heat. When butter melts and begins to bubble, add the egg mixture. Cook about 4 minutes or until no liquid remains, but eggs are still moist. Using the silicone or wooden spatula, stir about every 10 seconds. Remove from heat. Turn off burner.

4 Divide eggs among toast cups. Top with salsa, cheese, and tomatoes. Serve right away.

PER SERVING: 264 cal., 13 g fat (5 g sat. fat), 277 mg chol., 721 mg sodium, 24 g carb., 3 g fiber, 15 g pro.

 X1 X1 X½

KNOW IT

The average hen in America produces 250 to 300 eggs each year.

KARATE CHOP ENERGY BARS

These fruit- and oat-filled bars help fuel your endurance to power you through any challenge. Hi-yah!

MAKES: 16 servings

Ingredients

- ⅓ cup sliced almonds
- 1½ cups regular rolled oats
- 1 egg
- 1 banana, peeled
- ¼ cup almond butter or peanut butter
- ¼ cup honey
- ¼ cup whole wheat flour
- 1 teaspoon baking powder
- 1 teaspoon apple pie spice
- ½ teaspoon vanilla
- ¼ teaspoon salt
- 1½ cups puffed seven-grain and sesame cereal
- ½ cup dried apples, snipped into small pieces
- ¼ cup dried apricots, snipped into small pieces

Tools

Measuring cups, measuring spoons, kitchen scissors, 9x9x2-inch baking pan, foil, small resealable plastic bag, rolling pin, 15x10x1-inch baking pan, hot pads, wire cooling rack, large bowl, wire whisk, fork, wooden spoon, knife

Let's Make It!

1 Turn on the oven to 350°F. Line the 9x9x2-inch baking pan with foil, letting the foil hang over the edges of the pan. Set aside.

2 Put almonds in the plastic bag. Seal bag and use the rolling pin to crush almonds into small pieces. Spread almonds and oats in the 15x10x1-inch baking pan. Bake about 8 minutes or until lightly toasted. Use hot pads to remove pan from oven. Put pan on the wire rack and let cool.

3 Put egg into the large bowl. Lightly beat egg with the wire whisk. Mash banana with a fork. Add mashed banana, almond butter, honey, flour, baking powder, apple pie spice, vanilla, and salt to egg in bowl. Whisk until well mixed.

4 Add cereal, dried fruit, and cooled oats and almonds to bowl. Stir until combined. Spoon mixture evenly into foil-lined baking pan.

5 Bake about 20 minutes or until brown around edges. Turn off oven. Use the hot pads to remove pan from oven. Put pan on wire rack to cool. When completely cooled, use edges of foil to lift uncut bars from the pan. Cut into 16 bars.

PER BAR: 134 cal., 5 g fat (1 g sat. fat), 13 mg chol., 85 mg sodium, 20 g carb., 2 g fiber, 4 g pro.

X ½   X ½

MOVE IT!

Pretend you're a superhero fighting evil villains. Punch the air 30 times, alternating arms each time.

BERRY BLAST SMOOTHIE

MAKES: 4 (1¼-cup) servings

Ingredients

- 4 cups fresh or frozen mixed berries
- 1 12.3-ounce package (1½ cups) silken-style tofu (fresh bean curd)
- 1 cup unsweetened cranberry-raspberry juice
- ¼ cup flaxseed meal
- 3 tablespoons honey

  Fresh raspberries and/or blueberries (optional)

Tools

Measuring cups, measuring spoons, blender, 4 tall glasses

Jet to the kitchen for a berry-boosted smoothie blended to lip-smacking perfection in a flash.

Let's Make It!

1 Put the mixed berries, tofu, juice, flaxseed meal, and honey in the blender. Cover blender with lid. Blend on high speed until smooth. Pour into the glasses. If you like, top each glass with fresh raspberries and/or blueberries.

PER SMOOTHIE: 242 cal., 5 g fat (1 g sat. fat), 0 mg chol., 50 mg sodium, 42 g carb., 7 g fiber, 9 g pro.

 X2 X1

MOVE IT!
Time yourself running a lap around the yard. Try to get faster each time until you reach super speed!

Ace lunchtime with these lunch box recipes that make the grade. Prepare your meal the night before, pack it up, and tote to the cafeteria table. It's as easy as A, B, C.

A+ LUNCHES

USE-YOUR-NOODLE SALAD

If you're feeling like you have your wires crossed, reboot with a chilled pasta salad to keep you functioning at high speed.

MAKES: 1 serving

Ingredients

- 2 ounces rice sticks (rice noodles) or fettuccine, broken in half
- ¼ cup snow peas, ends cut off and each cut in half crosswise
- ¼ cup chopped cooked chicken
- 12 drained canned mandarin orange sections
- 4 drained canned pineapple chunks
- 2 tablespoons bottled light Asian dressing

Tools

Measuring cups, measuring spoons, cutting board, sharp knife, can opener, colander, medium saucepan, hot pads, pint airtight storage container, small airtight storage container, plastic fork, insulated lunch bag, ice pack

Let's Make It!

1 The night before serving, cook rice noodles following package directions. Put colander in sink. When noodles are cooked, add snow peas to saucepan. Turn off burner. Using hot pads, carefully pour noodles and peas into colander to drain. Rinse with cold water and let drain.

2 Put noodles and peas in the pint storage container. Top noodle mixture with chicken, oranges, and pineapple. Cover and seal. Put dressing into the small storage container. Cover and seal. Put in refrigerator until chilled or up to 12 hours.

3 To tote, pack containers and plastic fork in an insulated lunch bag with ice pack. Seal bag. At lunch, uncover noodle salad. Shake up dressing. Open dressing and pour over salad.

PER SERVING: 383 cal., 8 g fat (2 g sat. fat), 31 mg chol., 426 mg sodium, 63 g carb., 2 g fiber, 13 g pro.

X1   X2   X½

RECESS WRAPS

Take a break from the same boring sandwich with two totally different wraps that will help you hit the playground running.

Ingredients

- 2 ounces cooked ham, chopped
- ¼ cup drained canned pineapple tidbits
- ¼ cup chopped sweet red pepper
- 1 tablespoon sweet-and-sour sauce
- 2 leaves butterhead (Bibb or Boston) lettuce or romaine lettuce

Tools

Cutting board, sharp knife, fine-mesh sieve or colander, small bowl, wooden spoon, storage containers, insulated lunch bag, plastic spoon, ice pack

Let's Make It!

1 Put ham, pineapple, sweet pepper, and sweet-and-sour sauce in the small bowl. Stir to mix well with wooden spoon. Spoon into a storage container. Put lettuce in another storage container. Cover and seal. Put in refrigerator until chilled or up to 12 hours.

2 To tote, place containers and plastic spoon in the insulated lunch bag with ice pack. Seal bag. To serve, spoon ham mixture into lettuce leaves.

Tip: Serve with pretzel sticks and honey mustard dip.

PER SERVING: 214 cal., 6 g fat (2 g sat. fat), 32 mg chol., 803 mg sodium, 28 g carb., 6 g fiber, 14 g pro.

X2 X½

Ingredients

- 1   6- to 7-inch whole wheat tortilla or oval multigrain wrap
- 1   lettuce leaf, cut into shreds
- 4   grape tomatoes or cherry tomatoes, chopped
- ¼   cup shredded cooked chicken
- 2   tablespoons shredded reduced-fat cheddar cheese
- 2   pieces refrigerated jarred mango, cut into small pieces
- 2   tablespoons bottled light ranch salad dressing

Tools

Measuring cups, measuring spoons, cutting board, sharp knife, shredder, 12x12-inch piece waxed paper or parchment paper, airtight storage containers, plastic spoon, insulated lunch bag, ice pack

Let's Make It!

1 The night before serving, put tortilla on the waxed paper or parchment paper. Put lettuce in a line a little below the middle of the tortilla. Put tomatoes on lettuce. Top tomatoes with chicken and cheese.

2 Fold the bottom of the tortilla up and over filling. Roll up tortilla to make a log shape. Wrap the waxed paper or parchment paper around the tortilla wrap. Cut wrap in half across.

3 Put wrap in a storage container. Cover and seal. Put mango in a small storage container. Cover and seal. Put ranch dressing in a separate small storage container. Cover and seal.

4 Put containers and the plastic spoon in the insulated lunch bag. Seal bag. Put in refrigerator until chilled or up to 12 hours.

5 To tote, add ice pack to lunch bag. Seal bag. At lunch, remove paper from wrap. Use ranch dressing as a dip for the wrap.

PER SERVING: 378 cal., 14 g fat (3 g sat. fat), 48 mg chol., 748 mg sodium, 49 g carb., 8 g fiber, 22 g pro.

 X1 X1 X½

35

GEOMETRY SANDWICHES

Shape up your sandwich! Whatever angle you choose, this sandwich is the perfect lunchtime solution.

Ingredients

- 2 tablespoons favorite flavor hummus
- 2 slices whole grain bread
- 2 tablespoons purchased shredded carrot
- 6 thin slices seedless cucumber
- 1 slice reduced-fat Swiss or American cheese (about 1 ounce)
- 1 slice deli turkey breast or ham (about 1 ounce)
- ½ cup melon (watermelon, cantaloupe, and/or honeydew melon) cut into shapes such as balls, triangles, and/or cubes, or cut out with cookie cutters

Tools

Measuring cups, measuring spoons, cutting board, sharp knife, melon baller or cookie cutters (if you like), table knife, airtight storage containers, plastic fork, insulated lunch bag, ice pack

Let's Make It!

1 The night before serving, spread hummus on 1 slice of the bread. Top hummus with carrot and lightly press carrot into hummus. Arrange cucumber slices over carrot. Top with cheese and turkey. Top with the remaining slice of bread.

2 Cut sandwich in half. Cut one half of the sandwich into 2 triangles. Cut the other half of the sandwich into squares and/or rectangles. Arrange pieces in a storage container. Cover and seal.

3 Put melon in another storage container. Cover and seal. Put melon, sandwich, and plastic fork in the insulated lunch bag. Seal bag. Put in refrigerator until chilled or up to 12 hours.

4 To tote, add ice pack to lunch bag. Seal bag.

PER SERVING: 300 cal., 7 g fat (2 g sat. fat), 22 mg chol., 682 mg sodium, 41 g carb., 5 g fiber, 21 g pro.

X2 X2 X1 X½

KNOW IT!
Slicers and picklers are the two main varieties of cucumbers. Slicers are served fresh and picklers are made into pickles.

SCIENCE LAB CUP-O'-SOUP

Add a small school of cheesy fish to this swimmingly good soup for a lunch that makes a huge splash in the cafeteria.

MAKES: 1 serving + leftovers

Ingredients

- 1 tablespoon olive oil
- 1 large onion, chopped
- 1 carrot, peeled and chopped
- 1 stalk celery, chopped
- 2 cloves garlic, chopped
- 2 14.5-ounce cans no-salt-added diced tomatoes, undrained
- 1 14.5-ounce can reduced-sodium chicken broth
- 2 tablespoons snipped fresh basil
- 1 tablespoon lemon juice
- 1 teaspoon sugar
- 10 fish-shape cheese crackers
- 1 tablespoon chocolate-hazelnut spread
- 14 small square alphabet cookies
- 1 small apple

Tools

Measuring spoons, cutting board, sharp knife, vegetable peeler, can opener, kitchen scissors, large saucepan with lid, wooden spoons, blender, airtight storage containers, snack-size resealable plastic bag, single-serving thermos with lid, small saucepan, table knife, plastic spoon, insulated lunch bag

Let's Make It!

1 The night before serving, pour oil into the large saucepan. Put pan on burner. Turn burner to medium-high heat. Add onion, carrot, celery, and garlic. Cook for 5 minutes. Use a wooden spoon to stir every now and again.

2 Add tomatoes, broth, basil, lemon juice, and sugar to saucepan. Bring to boiling. Turn burner down to medium-low heat. Cover the pan with the lid. Cook about 20 minutes or until veggies are very tender. Stir every now and again. Use hot pads to remove pan from burner. Place pan on a hot mat. Turn off burner. Let mixture cool for 10 minutes.

3 Carefully pour soup into the blender. Put lid on blender. Blend on high speed until smooth. Pour into a storage container. Cover and seal and put in refrigerator. Put crackers in the snack-size bag. Seal bag.

4 In the morning, fill a single-serving thermos with very hot water. Put 1 cup of the soup in the small saucepan. Put pan on burner. Turn burner to medium-high heat. Cook until heated through. Use a wooden spoon to stir every now and again. Turn off burner. Pour hot water out of the thermos. Pour in the hot soup. Put lid on thermos right away. (Save the remaining soup for another lunch by refrigerating for up to 3 days or freezing for up to 3 months.)

5 Spread the chocolate-hazelnut spread over 7 of the cookies. Top with the remaining 7 cookies to make cookie sandwiches. Put in a storage container.

6 Pack thermos, crackers, apple, cookies, and the plastic spoon in the lunch bag. Seal bag.

PER SERVING: 353 cal., 9 g fat (2 g sat. fat), 1 mg chol., 420 mg sodium, 62 g carb., 6 g fiber, 6 g pro.

 X ½   X 1   X 1

ART CLASS BRUSHES

Dip into your painter's palette to create delicious works of art, then roll up the canvas and chow down!

MAKES: 1 serving

Ingredients

- 1   stalk celery, cut into 3- to 4-inch-long sticks
- 2   sticks mozzarella (string) cheese (about 2 ounces)
- 1   small carrot, peeled and cut into 3- to 4-inch-long sticks
- 2   ounces deli-sliced turkey breast
- 1   oval multigrain wrap
- 1   tablespoon bottled light ranch salad dressing
- 1   tablespoon ketchup
- 1   tablespoon yellow mustard

Tools

Measuring spoons, cutting board, sharp knife, vegetable peeler, medium bowl, ice, plastic wrap, small individual disposable containers with lids, insulated lunch bag, ice pack

Let's Make It!

1 The night before serving, make several small ½-inch-long cuts at one end of each celery stick. Place celery sticks in a bowl of ice water and let stand for several minutes so the ends spread out, forming "brushes." Separate strands of cheese at one end of each stick so cheese sticks also resemble brushes. Wrap celery, cheese, and carrot sticks separately in plastic wrap.

2 Lay sliced turkey on top of the multigrain wrap. Roll up loosely into a spiral. Wrap in plastic wrap.

3 Put ranch dressing, ketchup, and mustard in separate disposable containers. Cover and seal. Place carrot and celery sticks, cheese, sandwich wrap, and containers of spreads in an insulated lunch bag. Seal bag. Put in refrigerator until chilled or up to 12 hours.

4 To tote, add ice pack to lunch bag. Seal bag. At lunch, unroll sandwich wrap. Use the carrot and celery sticks and the cheese sticks to "paint" spreads on sandwich. Place the cheese sticks on top of the turkey. Roll into a spiral for eating. If you like, dip carrot and celery sticks into remaining spreads and eat with sandwich.

PER SERVING: 431 cal., 20 g fat (8 g sat. fat), 57 mg chol., 1,901 mg sodium, 40 g carb., 9 g fiber, 35 g pro.

X2   X1   X2   X1

WHEELS-ON-THE-BUS PASTA SALAD

This Southwest-inspired pasta salad will get your wheels spinning again and transport you back to class fully fueled.

MAKES: 1 serving

Ingredients

- ⅓ cup dried small wagon wheel pasta
- ⅓ cup rinsed and drained canned black beans
- ¼ cup fresh or frozen whole kernel corn
- ¼ cup halved cherry tomatoes
- 1 tablespoon light ranch salad dressing
- ⅛ to ¼ teaspoon chili powder
- 1 4.25-ounce container diced peaches in light syrup

Tools

Measuring cups, measuring spoons, can opener, cutting board, sharp knife, small saucepan, colander, hot pads, medium bowl, spoons, small bowl, airtight storage container, plastic spoon, insulated lunch bag, ice pack

Let's Make It!

1 Cook pasta following package directions. Put colander in the sink. Using hot pads, carefully pour pasta into colander to drain. Rinse with cold water and let drain.

2 Put pasta, beans, corn, and tomatoes in the medium bowl. Stir to mix. Put ranch dressing and chili powder in the small bowl. Stir to mix. Pour dressing mixture over pasta mixture. Stir until all ingredients are coated. Spoon into the storage container. Cover and seal. Put in refrigerator until chilled or up to 12 hours.

3 To tote, put storage container with salad, container with peaches, and plastic spoon in the lunch bag with an ice pack. Seal bag.

PER SERVING: 336 cal., 4 g fat (0 g sat. fat), 4 mg chol., 486 mg sodium, 69 g carb., 8 g fiber, 11 g pro.

X1   X1   X½   X½

MOVE IT!
After you get off the bus at home, build an obstacle course with friends and take turns racing through.

ALL-STAR SUPPERS

It's time for the main event—dinner! Show off your cooking skills and become the kitchen MVP with meals your whole family will cheer for. With macaroni and cheese, burritos, and meat loaf, every recipe is a touchdown.

BALANCE BEAM BURRITOS

The judges (your family) are sure to award you a perfect 10 for this balanced meal.

MAKES: 6 servings

Ingredients

1 cup leftover or purchased cooked brown rice

1 cup shredded cooked chicken

6 7- to 8-inch whole wheat tortillas

½ cup canned refried beans

2 tablespoons water

½ cup salsa

⅓ cup grape tomatoes, each cut in half

2 leaves romaine lettuce, chopped or cut into shreds

¼ cup shredded reduced-fat cheddar cheese (1 ounce)

Salsa and/or light sour cream

Tools

Measuring cups, measuring spoons, can opener, cutting board, sharp knife, shredder, spoons, 9-inch pie plate, foil, small saucepan, wooden spoon, hot pads

Let's Make It!

1 Turn on the oven to 350°F. Spoon rice into one half of the pie plate. Spoon chicken into the other half of the pie plate. Cover with foil. Wrap tortillas tightly in foil. Put pie plate and tortillas into oven. Bake for 10 to 15 minutes or until heated through.

2 Meanwhile, put refried beans and the water in the small saucepan. Stir to mix well. Put pan on burner. Turn burner to medium heat. Cook for 2 to 3 minutes or until heated through. Using the wooden spoon, stir every now and again. Turn burner down to low heat.

3 Use hot pads to remove pie plate and tortillas from oven. Turn off oven. Carefully open tortillas.

4 Layer beans, rice, chicken, the ½ cup salsa, the tomatoes, lettuce, and cheese in the center of the bottom half of each tortilla.

5 Fold bottom of each tortilla over filling. Fold in sides of tortilla over filling. Using both hands, roll tortilla away from you to enclose filling. Serve right away. If you like, serve with some more salsa and/or sour cream.

PER BURRITO: 251 cal., 7 g fat (2 g sat. fat), 23 mg chol., 600 mg sodium, 28 g carb., 12 g fiber, 18 g pro.

 X 1½   X 1½

MOVE IT!
Stretch a long piece of masking tape across the floor to make a balance beam. Dance and jump on it without falling off.

47

GOLD CUP BROCCOLI SLAW

MAKES: 4 to 5 (about 1-cup) servings

Be sure your defenders are ready! The kicked-up flavor of this crunchy slaw will bring fans running in from the sidelines.

Ingredients

¼ cup plain low-fat yogurt

2 teaspoons cider vinegar

¼ teaspoon salt

2 tablespoons chopped green onion (1)

2 oranges, cut in half (4 halves total)

1 small head broccoli, stem cut off and broccoli cut into small pieces (about 3 cups)

½ cup purchased shredded carrots

¼ cup golden raisins

¼ cup unsalted cashew pieces, toasted, if you like

Tools

Measuring cups, measuring spoons, cutting board, sharp knife, shredder, citrus juicer, medium serving bowl, large spoon, plastic wrap

Let's Make It!

1 Combine yogurt, vinegar, and salt in the serving bowl. Finely shred 1 teaspoon orange peel from one orange half, set aside. Juice 1 tablespoon from the same orange half, set aside. Add green onion, orange peel, and orange juice to yogurt mixture. Stir to mix. Peel remaining 3 orange halves and cut into small pieces. Add orange pieces, broccoli, carrots, and raisins to the mixture. Stir until evenly coated.

2 Cover bowl with plastic wrap and put in the refrigerator about 30 minutes or until chilled.

3 When ready to serve, stir to mix well. If you like, top with cashews.

PER SERVING: 99 cal., 1 g fat (0 g sat. fat), 1 mg chol., 186 mg sodium, 23 g carb., 4 g fiber, 4 g pro.

SUPER CHILI BOWL

Tackle even the biggest hunger when you rush this bowl packed with meat, beans, and veggies to the table.

MAKES: 4 (1½-cup) servings

Ingredients

Nonstick cooking spray

- 2 7- to 8-inch flour tortillas, cut into ½-inch-wide strips
- 8 ounces extra-lean ground beef
- 1 small onion, chopped
- 1 teaspoon chili powder
- 1 15-ounce can chili beans in chili gravy, undrained
- 1 14.5-ounce can diced tomatoes, undrained
- 1 8-ounce can tomato sauce
- 1 4-ounce can chopped green chile peppers, undrained
- 1 cup frozen whole kernel corn
- ½ cup shredded reduced-fat cheddar cheese (2 ounces)

Light sour cream, if you like

Tools

Measuring cups, measuring spoons, cutting board, sharp knife, pizza cutter (if you like to cut tortillas), can opener, shredder, baking sheet, hot pads, wire cooling rack, large saucepan, wide metal spatula

Let's Make It!

1 Turn on the oven to 375°F. Lightly coat the baking sheet with cooking spray. Put tortilla strips on baking sheet; lightly coat with cooking spray. Bake for 7 to 8 minutes or until crisp and light brown. Turn off oven. Use hot pads to remove baking sheet from oven. Put baking sheet on the wire rack and cool completely.

2 Coat the large saucepan with cooking spray. Put saucepan on burner. Turn burner to medium-high heat. Add beef, onion, and chili powder to saucepan. Cook about 8 minutes or until vegetables are tender and beef is cooked through. Use the spatula to stir every now and again and to break up meat as it cooks.

3 Pour chili beans, tomatoes, tomato sauce, and chile peppers into the meat mixture in the saucepan. Add corn to saucepan. Bring to boiling. Turn burner down to medium-low heat. Cook about 20 minutes or until as thick as you like it. Use spatula to stir every now and again. Turn off burner.

4 Serve chili topped with cheddar cheese, tortilla "goalpost" strips, and, if you like, sour cream.

PER SERVING: 397 cal., 11 g fat (4 g sat. fat), 45 mg chol., 1,099 mg sodium, 49 g carb., 9 g fiber, 26 g pro.

X 3½   X ½   X 1

SLAM DUNK CHEESE SAUCE

Veggies dunked in this slammin' sauce will keep you light on your feet for serious air time.

MAKES: 6 (¼-cup) servings

Ingredients

- 1 cup fat-free milk
- 1 tablespoon all-purpose flour
- 2 ounces reduced-fat cream cheese (Neufchâtel), softened
- 1 cup shredded reduced-fat cheddar cheese (4 ounces)
- 2 teaspoons Dijon-style mustard
- 3 cups hot cooked vegetables, such as broccoli, carrots, and/or cauliflower

Tools

Measuring cups, measuring spoons, shredder, medium glass jar with screw-top lid, small saucepan, wooden spoon, hot pads, hot mat

Let's Make It!

1 Put milk and flour in the jar. Tightly screw lid on jar. Shake jar until mixture is completely smooth (no lumps of flour). Pour mixture into the saucepan. Put saucepan on burner. Turn burner to medium-high heat. Cook about 5 minutes or until sauce bubbles and thickens. Use the wooden spoon to stir all the time.

2 Turn burner down to low heat. Use hot pads to remove saucepan from heat. Place saucepan on hot mat. Add cream cheese, cheddar cheese, and mustard. Stir until cheese is all melted and sauce is smooth. Return to burner and keep warm. Stir every now and again. Turn off burner.

3 Serve sauce with the cooked vegetables.

PER SERVING: 120 cal., 6 g fat (4 g sat. fat), 21 mg chol., 238 mg sodium, 9 g carb., 2 g fiber, 8 g pro.

 X1 ⬤ X½

MOVE IT!

Swap a basketball hoop for a Hula-Hoop! Compete with friends to see who can hoop the longest.

FOOTBALL MEAT LOAF

Hike this hearty dish to the kitchen table and everyone will happily play a receiver.

Ingredients

Nonstick cooking spray
- 2 ounces deli-sliced part-skim mozzarella cheese
- 1 egg
- ⅓ cup quick-cooking rolled oats
- ⅓ cup purchased shredded carrot
- ¼ cup panko (Japanese-style bread crumbs)
- 3 tablespoons fat-free milk
- 2 tablespoons grated Parmesan cheese
- 1 tablespoon dried minced onion
- 1 teaspoon dried Italian seasoning, crushed
- ½ teaspoon garlic powder
- 1½ pounds uncooked ground chicken or turkey breast
- ⅓ cup pasta sauce or barbecue sauce

Tools

Measuring cups, measuring spoons, shredder, 2-quart rectangular baking dish, cutting board, sharp knife, plastic wrap, large bowl, fork, large spoons, ruler, instant-read thermometer, hot pads, hot mat

Let's Make It!

1 Turn on the oven to 350°F. Lightly coat the baking dish with cooking spray. Set aside.

2 Put 1 slice of the mozzarella cheese on a cutting board. Cut three ¼-inch-wide strips off the edge of the cheese slice. Wrap strips in plastic wrap and put in the refrigerator. Chop the remaining mozzarella cheese.

3 Put egg into the large bowl. Lightly beat egg with the fork. Add the chopped mozzarella cheese, the rolled oats, carrot, panko, milk, Parmesan cheese, dried onion, Italian seasoning, and garlic powder. Stir to mix well. Add chicken and stir to mix well.

4 Put the chicken mixture into the prepared baking dish. Use your clean hands to shape it into a football shape about 2 inches thick.

5 Bake about 45 minutes or until an instant-read thermometer inserted into the center registers 160°F. Use hot pads to remove baking dish from oven. Spoon pasta sauce over the meat loaf. Bake for 5 minutes more. Turn off oven. Use hot pads to remove baking dish from oven. Place baking dish on hot mat.

6 Carefully arrange reserved cheese strips down the center of the top of the meat loaf to resemble football laces, cutting strips as needed. Let stand for 10 minutes before slicing.

PER SERVING: 260 cal., 13 g fat (5 g sat. fat), 139 mg chol., 232 mg sodium, 9 g carb., 1 g fiber, 26 g pro.

 X3   X½

55

GAME DAY GOULASH

Whether you're fueling up for a game or cheering from the stands, the team of pasta, meat, and veggies is a winner.

Tools

Measuring cups, measuring spoons, cutting board, sharp knife, can opener, large saucepan, colander, large skillet, wooden spoon

Ingredients

Nonstick cooking spray

1 pound uncooked ground turkey or chicken

1 red sweet pepper, stem cut off, seeds removed, and chopped

1 small onion, chopped

½ cup packaged coarsely shredded carrots

1 tablespoon all-purpose flour

2 teaspoons sweet paprika

1 14.5-ounce can diced tomatoes with basil, garlic, and oregano, undrained

1 8-ounce can no-salt-added tomato sauce

½ cup reduced-sodium chicken broth

8 ounces dried multigrain elbow macaroni, cooked following package directions and drained

Sour cream, if you like

Let's Make It!

1 Lightly coat the large skillet with cooking spray. Put on burner. Turn burner to medium-high heat. Add turkey, sweet pepper, onion, and carrots. Cook about 6 minutes or until vegetables are tender and turkey is brown. Use the wooden spoon to stir every now and again and to break up turkey while it cooks.

2 Sprinkle flour and paprika over mixture in skillet. Cook for 2 minutes, stirring every now and again. Add tomatoes, tomato sauce, and broth to skillet. Cook and stir until mixture starts to boil. Turn burner down to medium heat. Cook about 5 minutes or until mixture has thickened slightly. Turn off burner.

3 Serve turkey mixture over hot cooked macaroni. If you like, top with sour cream.

PER SERVING: 248 cal., 5 g fat (1 g sat. fat), 45 mg chol., 341 mg sodium, 33 g carb., 3 g fiber, 16 g pro.

X 1½   X 1   X ½

BAKED POTATO BOULDERS

Rope together ingredients for your favorite flavor option. No matter how you top them, these spuds rock!

MAKES: 4 servings

Ingredients

2   large baking potatoes (about 8 ounces each)
1   choice Stir-in and Topper

Tools

Vegetable brush, fork, 13x9x2-inch baking pan, hot pads, sharp knife, cooking spoon, potato masher or fork, foil, large metal spatula, measuring cups, measuring spoons

Let's Make It!

1 Turn oven to 375°F. Scrub potatoes with a vegetable brush under running cool water. Use a fork to poke potatoes in several places. Place potatoes in a 13x9x2-inch baking pan.

2 Place pan in oven and bake for 1 hour or until tender when poked with a fork.* While potatoes are baking prepare Stir-in and Topper. When potatoes are tender, use hot pads to remove pan from the oven.

3 When potatoes are cool enough to handle, use a sharp knife to cut potatoes in half lengthwise to create 4 boat-shape pieces. Use a spoon to remove potato pulp from halves. Leave about a ¼-inch thickness of potato attached to the skins. Place the potato pulp in a medium mixing bowl.

4 Using a potato masher or fork, mash potato pulp. Add your Stir-in to bowl. Using a wooden spoon, mix well. Spoon mixture into potato skins.* Return potato halves to baking pan. Cover with foil. Put pan in oven and bake for 15 to 20 minutes until heated through.

5 Turn off oven. Use hot pads to carefully remove baking pan from oven. With a spatula put potatoes on plates. Divide Topper over potatoes.

*Tip: Potatoes can be prepared to this point, covered and refrigerated until ready to finish. Add another 5 to 10 minute to baking time if potatoes are cold.

Creamy Ham and Broccoli

Stir-in: ½ cup diced low-sodium ham; ¾ cup chopped cooked broccoli; ¼ cup fat-free milk; ¼ cup reduced-fat cream cheese, softened; and ¼ teaspoon salt.

Topper: ¼ cup shredded low-fat mozzarella cheese and, if you like, 2 tablespoons snipped fresh parsley.

PER SERVING: 191 cal., 6 g fat (3 g sat. fat), 27 mg chol., 460 mg sodium, 23 g carb., 4 g fiber, 12 g pro.

 X ½ X 1

Pizza Potatoes

Stir-in: ½ cup chopped low-fat turkey pepperoni; ½ cup chopped green sweet pepper; ¼ cup fat-free milk; and ¼ teaspoon salt.

Topper: ¼ cup warmed pizza sauce and ¼ cup shredded pizza cheese.

PER SERVING: 179 cal., 4 g fat (2 g sat. fat), 32 mg chol., 628 mg sodium, 24 g carb., 3 g fiber, 12 g pro.

 X ½ X 1

Chicken Nachos

Stir-in: 1 cup chopped cooked chicken; ⅓ cup frozen corn, thawed; ¼ cup salsa; ¼ cup light sour cream; and ¼ teaspoon salt.

Topper: ¼ cup shredded reduced-fat cheddar cheese, ¼ cup chopped fresh tomato, and ¼ cup coarsely crushed tortilla chips.

PER SERVING: 223 cal., 6 g fat (2 g sat. fat), 39 mg chol., 415 mg sodium, 28 g carb., 3 g fiber, 15 g pro.

 X 1½ X 1

M.V.P. MAC'N' CHEESE

Keep this recipe in your starting lineup. It will quickly become your MVD (most valuable dinner).

MAKES: 4 (1½-cup) servings

Ingredients

8   ounces dried multigrain penne pasta (about 2⅔ cups dry)

2   cups frozen mixed vegetables

1⅔ cups fat-free milk

3   tablespoons all-purpose flour

4   ounces reduced-fat American cheese (about 6 slices), torn

1   cup shredded reduced-fat cheddar cheese (4 ounces)

1   cup chopped cooked turkey breast

1   cup chopped, seeded tomatoes

Tools

Measuring cups, measuring spoons, shredder, cutting board, sharp knife, large saucepan, wooden spoon, colander, hot pads

Let's Make It!

1 Fill the large saucepan three-fourths full with cool water. Put on burner. Turn burner to medium-high heat. Carefully add macaroni to saucepan. Cook following package directions. Use the wooden spoon to stir every now and again. About 4 minutes before macaroni should be done, add frozen vegetables to the saucepan. Bring back to boiling. Cook about 3 minutes more or until macaroni and vegetables are tender. Turn off burner. Place colander in sink. Using the hot pads, carefully pour macaroni and vegetables into colander to drain.

2 Put milk and flour in the same saucepan. Stir to mix well. Put pan on burner. Turn burner to medium-high heat. Cook until mixture starts to bubble. Cook for 2 minutes more. Use the wooden spoon to stir all of the time. Turn burner down to medium-low heat.

3 Using the wooden spoon, stir in the American cheese a little at a time. When mixture is smooth, stir in the cheddar cheese a little at a time.

4 When all the cheese is added and the sauce is smooth, add the macaroni and mixed vegetables, the turkey, and tomatoes. Cook and stir until heated through. Remove from heat. Turn off burner.

PER SERVING: 515 cal., 12 g fat (6 g sat. fat), 68 mg chol., 720 mg sodium, 61 g carb., 8 g fiber, 43 g pro.

 X 1½ X 2 X 1½ X 1

PITCHER'S MOUND POTATOES

Throw dinner guests a curve ball by serving delicious sweet potatoes topped with "dirt."

Ingredients

1   pound Yukon gold potatoes (about 3 medium), peeled and cut into 1-inch pieces

1   pound sweet potatoes (about 2 large), peeled and cut into 1-inch pieces

½   teaspoon salt

¼   cup low-fat milk

3   ounces reduced-fat cream cheese (Neufchâtel), softened, or ⅓ cup light sour cream

1   tablespoon butter

½   teaspoon salt

2   tablespoons flaxseed meal
    Butter, if you like

Tools

Measuring cups, measuring spoons, vegetable peeler, cutting board, sharp knife, colander, large saucepan with lid, fork, hot pads, hot mat, potato masher, wooden spoon, serving plate

Let's Make It!

1 Put colander in sink. Put potato pieces in colander and rinse with cold water.

2 Put potatoes in the large saucepan. Return colander to sink. Add enough cold water to saucepan to cover potatoes. Add ½ teaspoon salt to saucepan. Put pan on burner. Turn burner to high heat. When water starts to boil, turn burner down to medium-low heat. Put lid on saucepan. Cook about 10 minutes or until tender when poked with the fork. Turn off burner.

3 Using hot pads, pour potatoes into colander to drain. Put pan on the hot mat. Return potatoes to saucepan. Add milk, cream cheese, the 1 tablespoon butter, and ½ teaspoon salt.

4 Mash potato mixture until as smooth as you like. Pile up potatoes into a mound on the serving plate. Sprinkle flaxseed meal evenly over potato mound. If you like, top with additional butter.

PER SERVING: 190 cal., 6 g fat (3 g sat. fat), 16 mg chol., 481 mg sodium, 30 g carb., 4 g fiber, 4 g pro.

 X1

KNOW IT!

In 1995 potatoes became the first vegetable to be grown in space.

HIT-THE-SLOPES FRUIT SALAD

Build a sweet snow-topped mountain of fruit, grab a fork, and make your way down the slope.

Ingredients

- 1   8-ounce can crushed pineapple (packed in juice), well drained and pressed dry
- 1   6-ounce container plain or vanilla low-fat yogurt
- 12   fresh strawberries, tops cut off and each berry cut in half
- 1   large banana, peeled and cut into ¼-inch-thick slices
- 1   cup seedless red grapes, each cut in half
- 2   teaspoons lemon juice
- ¼   cup shredded coconut,* if you like

Tools

Measuring cups, measuring spoons, can opener, colander, large spoons, cutting board, sharp knife, small bowl, plastic wrap, medium serving bowl

Let's Make It!

1 Put pineapple in the small bowl and add yogurt. Stir to mix well. Cover with plastic wrap and chill in refrigerator until ready to serve.

2 Put strawberries in the serving bowl. Add banana and grapes to strawberries. Drizzle with lemon juice. Gently stir to mix well. Cover bowl with plastic wrap. Put in refrigerator about 30 minutes or until chilled.**

3 When ready to serve, remove plastic wrap. Gently stir fruit mixture. Stir yogurt mixture with another spoon and spoon over fruit.

Sprinkle coconut over salad if you are using it. If you like, gently stir to combine.

*Tip: If you want to use toasted coconut, turn on the oven to 350°F. Put coconut in a shallow baking pan, spreading into a thin layer. Using a wooden spoon and hot pads, stir once or twice during baking. Bake for 3 to 5 minutes or until golden brown. Turn off oven. Use hot pads to remove pan from oven. Place pan on a wire cooling rack and let cool.

**Tip: If you chill the fruit mixture too long the banana will turn brown.

PER SERVING: 134 cal., 1 g fat (0 g sat. fat), 3 mg chol., 32 mg sodium, 31 g carb., 3 g fiber, 3 g pro.

X1

"TRACK MEAT" PIES

Set a personal record when you clear the bar in just one try with this over-the-top dinner pie.

MAKES: 4 servings

Ingredients

- 1 rolled refrigerated unbaked piecrust (½ of a 15-ounce package)
- Nonstick cooking spray
- 12 ounces lean ground beef or uncooked ground chicken
- ½ of a small onion, chopped
- ½ cup chopped celery (1 stalk)
- 2 tablespoons all-purpose flour
- 1 cup reduced-sodium beef broth
- ½ teaspoon dried Italian seasoning, crushed
- ¼ teaspoon salt
- 2 cups frozen mixed vegetables

Tools

Measuring cups, measuring spoons, cutting board, sharp knife, large skillet, wooden spoon, colander, four 10-ounce individual casserole dishes, shallow baking pan, hot pads, wire cooling rack

Let's Make It!

1 Turn on the oven to 400°F. Let piecrust stand following package directions. Coat the large skillet with cooking spray. Put skillet on burner. Turn burner to medium-high heat. Add meat, onion, and celery to skillet. Cook about 8 minutes or until vegetables are tender and meat is cooked through. Use the wooden spoon to stir every now and again and to break up the meat as it cooks. Place colander in sink. Using hot pads, carefully pour meat mixture into colander to drain. Return meat mixture to the skillet.

2 Turn burner down to medium heat. Sprinkle flour over meat. Cook and stir to coat meat. Add broth, Italian seasoning, and salt. Bring to boiling. Cook until the mixture starts to thicken. Stir with the wooden spoon every now and again.

3 Add frozen vegetables to skillet. Return to boiling. Cook for 3 minutes. Stir every now and again. Turn off burner. Using hot pads, remove skillet from heat. Carefully spoon hot mixture into the individual casserole dishes.*

4 Unroll piecrust onto a cutting board. Using a sharp knife or pizza cutter, cut crust into 8 wedges. Put 2 wedges on each dish, placing pieces in opposite directions so they don't overlap. Place dishes in the shallow baking pan.

5 Bake about 20 minutes or until filling is bubbling and crust is golden brown. Turn off oven. Use hot pads to remove pan from oven. Place pan on the wire rack. Let pies cool for 5 minutes before serving. Makes 4 servings.

*Tip: If you do not have individual casseroles, you can make one bigger pie in a 9-inch pie plate. Do not cut the piecrust. Instead unroll and place the whole crust on the filling. Bake as directed in Step 5.

PER SERVING: 466 cal., 22 g fat (9 g sat. fat), 55 mg chol., 569 mg sodium, 43 g carb., 5 g fiber, 22 g pro.

 X2   X2   X1

67

TUMBLER TORTELLINI SALAD

Everyone will flip for this combo of pasta, chicken, and veggies!

Ingredients

1 9-ounce package refrigerated cheese-filled tortellini

2 small yellow and/or red sweet peppers, stems cut off, seeds removed, and cut into bite-size strips

½ of a small cucumber, peeled (if you like), seeds removed, and chopped

1 cup shredded purchased roasted chicken

½ cup grape tomatoes, each cut in half

¼ cup sliced pitted ripe olives

½ cup bottled reduced-calorie Italian dressing

¼ cup finely shredded Parmesan cheese

Let's Make It!

1 Cook tortellini in the large saucepan following package directions. Turn off burner. Place colander in sink. Using hot pads, carefully pour tortellini into colander to drain. Rinse with cold water and let drain.

2 Put tortellini, sweet peppers, cucumber, chicken, tomatoes, and olives in the serving bowl. Pour dressing over mixture. Stir to mix well. Cover with plastic wrap. Chill in the refrigerator for at least 2 hours or up to 24 hours.

3 When ready to serve, stir to mix well. Top with Parmesan.

PER SERVING: 293 cal., 11 g fat (3 g sat. fat), 47 mg chol., 566 mg sodium, 31 g carb., 3 g fiber, 18 g pro.

 X1 X1 X1

Tools

Measuring cups, cutting board, sharp knife, shredder, large saucepan, colander, hot pads, large serving bowl, wooden spoon, plastic wrap

SNACK ADVENTURES

Ready for some extreme snacks? Try a royal treat, shooting stars, or prehistoric munchies to keep you fueled for after-school adventures—wherever in the world they may take you.

ROCKET POPS

Beat a rumbling stomach and hot summer days with fruity, frosty treats that will lick hunger in 10, 9, 8 . . .

Ingredients

- 1 envelope unflavored gelatin
- ¼ cup sugar
- ½ cup water
- 2 cups chopped fresh strawberries or peeled peaches
- 1 6-ounce container vanilla low-fat yogurt
- ½ cup fat-free milk
- ½ cup pomegranate juice

Tools

Measuring cups, small saucepan, wooden spoon, hot mat, blender, 15 freezer pop molds or 3-ounce paper drink cups*

Let's Make It!

1 Put gelatin and sugar in the small saucepan. Stir to mix. Add the water and stir to mix well. Let stand for 5 minutes. Put saucepan on burner. Turn burner to medium heat. Cook until sugar dissolves, stirring every now and again. Turn off burner. Remove from heat and put on the hot mat. Cool completely.

2 Put strawberries, yogurt, milk, and juice in the blender. Add cooled gelatin mixture. Cover with lid. Blend on high speed until smooth.

Spoon into freezer pop molds or paper drink cups.* Freeze about 4 hours or until firm.

3 To serve, remove pops from molds** or cups.

*Tip: If using the drink cups, place filled cups in a 13x9x2-inch baking pan. Cover each cup with foil. Use a sharp knife to make a small hole in the center of each piece of foil. Slide a wooden pop stick through the hole into the fruit mixture in each cup.

**Tip: To remove the frozen pops from the molds, quickly run warm water over the surface of the molds. Remove from molds.

PER POP: 35 cal., 0 g fat, 1 mg chol., 13 mg sodium, 7 g carb., 0 g fiber, 1 g pro.

KNOW IT!
Strawberries are not considered true berries because their seeds are on the outside.

JEWELED GRANITA TREASURES

Ahoy, landlubber! Practice your pirate skills by digging up the sweet fruit treasures in this golden granita. Arr!

MAKES: 5 (1-cup) servings

Ingredients

- ⅓ cup sugar
- ⅓ cup water
- 1½ cups chopped, peeled mango
- 1½ cups chopped, peeled peaches
- 2 tablespoons fruit juice and/or vegetable juice
- ½ cup chopped seedless green and/or red grapes and/or chopped apple

Tools

Measuring cups, measuring spoons, small saucepan, wooden spoon, blender, 3-quart rectangular baking dish, rubber spatula, fork

MOVE IT!
Ask parents to hide items in the house or yard and give you clues to help you find them. See how quickly you can complete the treasure hunt.

Let's Make It!

1 Put sugar and the water in the small saucepan. Stir to mix well. Put saucepan on burner. Turn burner to medium heat. Cook until sugar dissolves, stirring every now and again. Remove from heat. Cool completely.

2 Put the sugar mixture, mango, peaches, and juice in the blender. Put lid on blender. Blend on high speed until smooth. Stir in grapes. Pour into the baking dish. Use the rubber spatula to scrape down sides of blender. Freeze about 1½ hours or until firm. Use the fork to scrape across the frozen mixture in dish to make chunky jewels. Freeze about 3 hours more or until frozen, scraping the mixture with the fork every 30 minutes.

PER SERVING: 57 cal., 0 g fat, 0 mg chol., 2 mg sodium, 15 g carb., 1 g fiber, 0 g pro.

 X1

WILD MONKEYS

MAKES: 1 serving

Ingredients

1 8-inch multigrain tortilla
    Butter-flavor nonstick cooking spray

1 teaspoon sugar

½ teaspoon ground cinnamon

6 thin slices banana

1½ tablespoons creamy reduced-fat peanut butter

1 to 2 tablespoons flaked coconut (optional)

    Whole almonds or semisweet chocolate pieces

    Raisins

If you've ever been told not to make faces, now's the chance to monkey around. Make a wild monkey face, then swing in to gobble it up.

KNOW IT!
A bunch of a bananas is called a hand. Each banana in the bunch is called a finger.

Tools

Measuring spoons, table knives, baking sheet, parchment paper, 3-inch round cookie cutter, 2-inch round cookie cutter, 1½-inch round cookie cutter, small bowl, hot pads, wire cooling rack

Let's Make It!

1 Turn on the oven to 400°F. Line a baking sheet with parchment paper. Using the round cutters, carefully cut two 3-inch rounds, one 2-inch round, and four 1½-inch rounds from the tortilla. Put rounds on the prepared baking sheet. Coat with cooking spray.

2 Combine sugar and cinnamon in the small bowl. Sprinkle sugar-cinnamon mixture over the tortilla rounds. Bake about 8 minutes or until crisp. Turn off oven. Use the hot pads to remove the baking sheet from oven. Put baking sheet on the wire rack. Cool completely.

3 Set aside 2 of the banana slices. Spread the 3-inch rounds with peanut butter and put the remaining 4 banana slices on one of the peanut butter-spread rounds. Turn the remaining peanut butter-spread round so the peanut butter is down and put it on top of these banana slices to create a sandwich.

4 Place the 2-inch round on the lower center portion of the sandwich for the snout, using some more peanut butter to glue the snout in place. Put two of the 1½-inch rounds on the upper portion of the sandwich for the eyes, using more peanut butter as glue. Spread these small rounds with peanut butter and sprinkle with coconut if you like. Put an almond or chocolate piece in the center of each for the eyes.

5 Insert the remaining two 1½-inch rounds on the left and right sides of the sandwich for ears. Spread some peanut butter on the reserved banana slices and place each banana slice, spread side down, in the center of a monkey ear. Using the remaining peanut butter as glue, arrange raisins on the snout to look like a mouth. If you like, add an almond, chocolate pieces, or raisins for a nose. Serve right away.

PER SERVING: 343 cal., 14 g fat (3 g sat. fat), 0 mg chol., 467 mg sodium, 39 g carb., 13 g fiber, 16 g pro.

🥄 X 1½   🍞 X 1

ROYAL FRUIT CROWNS

Crown yourself king or queen of the kitchen with these regal treats. Share with parents and siblings to create a royal family.

MAKES: 6 servings

Ingredients

Nonstick cooking spray
- 6 wonton wrappers
- 1 teaspoon sugar
- ½ teaspoon ground cinnamon
- 1 cup coarsely chopped honeydew melon
- 1 cup fresh raspberries
- ¾ cup fresh blueberries
- ½ cup coarsely chopped, peeled kiwifruit
- 1 tablespoon honey
- 1 tablespoon lime juice

Tools

Measuring cups, measuring spoons, cutting board, sharp knife, muffin pan with six 2½-inch muffin cups, very small bowl, spoons, hot pads, wire cooling rack, small thin-bladed knife, medium bowl, 6 dessert dishes

Let's Make It!

1 Turn on the oven to 375°F. For wonton crowns, lightly coat the muffin cups with cooking spray. Press each wonton wrapper into bottom and up the sides of 1 of the prepared cups, pressing to make sure wrappers stick to sides. Coat insides of wonton cups with cooking spray. Put the sugar and cinnamon in the very small bowl. Stir to mix. Sprinkle sugar-cinnamon mixture over the insides of the wonton cups.

2 Bake for 7 to 9 minutes or until golden brown and crisp. Turn off oven. Use hot pads to remove muffin pan from oven. Put pan on the wire rack. Cool completely. Using the thin-bladed knife, carefully remove wonton crowns from the muffin cups.

3 Meanwhile, put honeydew, raspberries, blueberries, and kiwifruit in the medium bowl. Drizzle fruit with honey and lime juice. Toss to coat.

4 To serve, divide the fruit mixture evenly among the dessert dishes. Top each with a wonton crown.

PER CROWN: 78 cal., 0 g fat, 1 mg chol., 52 mg sodium, 19 g carb., 3 g fiber, 2 g pro.

 X ½

MOVE IT!
Imagine you're a frog prince or princess stuck in frog form. Hop up and down like a frog 20 times.

GONE FISHIN' SNACK MIX

Lure everyone to the kitchen with this sweet and salty mix as bait.

Ingredients

- 1 cup bite-size fish-shape crackers
- 1 cup round toasted-oat cereal with nuts and honey
- 1 cup pretzel sticks or twists
- 1 cup raisins, dried tart cherries, dried cranberries, and/or chopped dried pineapple

Tools

Measuring cups, large bowl, large spoon, 8 snack-size resealable plastic bags

Let's Make It!

1 Put crackers, cereal, pretzels, and raisins in the large bowl. Stir to mix. Put ½ cup of the snack mix in each plastic bag. Seal bags. Store at room temperature for up to 2 weeks.

PER SERVING: 121 cal., 2 g fat (0 g sat. fat), 2 mg chol., 173 mg sodium, 26 g carb., 1 g fiber, 2 g pro.

X ½

BOOGIE BOARD BITES

These dunkable treats make a splash with pro boarders and doggie paddlers alike.

Ingredients

- 4 2.25-ounce tubes berry-flavor blue portable low-fat yogurt
- ½ cup fresh blueberries
- 2 whole graham cracker rectangles
- 1 ounce dark chocolate

Tools

Measuring cups, small bowl, small plate, small microwave-safe bowl, hot pads, spoons, small resealable plastic bag, scissors

Let's Make It!

1 Put yogurt and blueberries in the small bowl. Stir to mix well. Break graham crackers along the lines so that you have 8 small rectangles and place on the plate.

2 Put chocolate in the microwave-safe bowl. Microwave on 50 percent power (medium) for 30 seconds. Stir the chocolate. Repeat until chocolate is melted and smooth.

3 Scrape chocolate into the plastic bag. Seal bag. Use scissors to snip off a small corner of the bag. Squeeze bag to drizzle chocolate onto graham crackers. Serve blueberry-yogurt mixture as dip with the graham crackers.

PER SERVING: 135 cal., 4 g fat (2 g sat. fat), 1 mg chol., 70 mg sodium, 24 g carb., 1 g fiber, 3 g pro.

CHUCKWAGON CHIPS

Mosey on into the kitchen and wrangle the ingredients for midday chow.

82

Ingredients

¼ cup canned whole kernel corn

¼ cup drained canned black beans

1 small tomato, chopped

12 baked tortilla chips or scoop-shape tortilla chips

1 tablespoon light sour cream

Tools

Measuring cups, measuring spoons, can opener, cutting board, sharp knife, colander, medium bowl, spoon, serving plate, small resealable plastic bag, scissors

Let's Make It!

1 Put the colander in the sink and add the corn and black beans. Run water over the corn and beans until they are rinsed clean. Shake off any excess water.

2 Add the corn, beans, and tomato to the medium bowl. Stir to mix. Place the tortilla chips on the serving plate. Spoon corn mixture onto the tortilla chips. Put the sour cream in the plastic bag. Seal bag. Use the scissors to snip off a tiny corner of the bag. Squeeze out a little squiggle of sour cream onto each of the filled chips.

PER SERVING: 94 cal., 2 g fat (1 g sat. fat), 2 mg chol., 284 mg sodium, 17 g carb., 3 g fiber, 3 g pro.

X ½   X ½   X ½

KNOW IT!
The record for the heaviest tomato was set in 1986. The tomato weighed in at 7 pounds 12 ounces!

DINO EGGS

Full of veggies and fruit, this is a perfect snack for any herbivore, but carnivores will roar for it too!

MAKES: 1 serving

Ingredients

- 1 cup packaged shredded cabbage and carrots (coleslaw mix)
- ¼ cup vanilla low-fat yogurt
- 1 tablespoon dried cranberries
- 5 seedless green grapes
- 5 seedless red grapes

Tools

Measuring cups, measuring spoons, small bowl, large spoon, salad plate

Let's Make It!

1 Pour the coleslaw mix into the small bowl. Add yogurt and dried cranberries. Stir to mix.

2 Spoon the coleslaw mixture onto the plate, spreading it into a circle to look like a nest. Place the grapes in the center to look like eggs.

PER SERVING: 129 cal., 1 g fat (1 g sat. fat), 4 mg chol., 54 mg sodium, 28 g carb., 2 g fiber, 4 g pro.

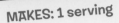 X ½   X 1

JURASSIC JUICE

MAKES: 2 (1-cup) servings

Ingredients

1 large banana, peeled and cut in half lengthwise

½ cup banana-, mango-, or pineapple-flavor yogurt

½ cup unsweetened pineapple juice

1 cup ice cubes

The evolution from banana, yogurt, and juice to slurpable smoothie is one of the fastest ever.

Tools

Measuring cups, cutting board, table knife, blender or food processor, 2 tall glasses, rubber spatula, 2 straws

Let's Make It!

1 Put 1 of the banana halves in the blender or food processor. Add the yogurt and pineapple juice to the blender or food processor. Add the ice. Cover and blend or process until smooth. Pour into glasses. Use the rubber spatula to scrape down the sides. Cut the remaining banana half into slices. Skewer the slices onto the straws. Place the straws in the glasses as a garnish.

PER SERVING: 166 cal., 1 g fat (1 g sat. fat), 2 mg chol., 38 mg sodium, 38 g carb., 2 g fiber, 4 g pro.

 X1

SHOOTING STAR BITES

If your stomach feels like a black hole, fill it with your favorite flavor from this constellation.

Ingredients

1   slice whole wheat bread
    Assorted Toppers

Tools

Toaster, star cookie cutter(s),
measuring spoons, small bowl,
spoons, table knife, cutting board,
sharp knife, shredder (if needed)

Let's Make It!

1 Use cookie cutter(s) to cut toast into star shapes. Top stars with your Topper choice.

Strawberry Stars: Use a spoon to mix 1 tablespoon light cream cheese and ¼ teaspoon cinnamon in a small bowl. Spread on the toast stars using a table knife. Place 2 medium strawberries on a cutting board and use a sharp knife to cut the green tops off of each strawberry. Slice the strawberries into bite-size pieces. Sprinkle the strawberries on the toast stars.

PER SERVING: 92 calories, 3 g fat (2 g sat. fat), 8 mg chol., 176 mg sodium, 12 g carb., 2 g fiber, 4 g pro.

 X 1

Blueberry-Nut Stars: Use a table knife to spread 1 tablespoon light blueberry cream cheese on toast stars. Sprinkle 3 tablespoons fresh blueberries and 1 teaspoon chopped walnuts on top.

PER SERVING: 119 calories, 4 g fat (2 g sat. fat), 8 mg chol., 161 mg sodium, 16 g carb., 2 g fiber, 4 g pro.

 X 1

Ranch-Style Stars: Use a spoon to mix 1 tablespoon light cream cheese and 1 teaspoon bottled Ranch dressing in a small bowl. Spread on the toast stars. Sprinkle tops with 1 tablespoon shredded carrot.

PER SERVING: 109 calories, 5 g fat (2 g sat. fat), 9 mg chol., 218 mg sodium, 11 g carb., 2 g fiber, 4 g pro.

 X 1

Taco Stars: Use a spoon to mix 1 tablespoon light cream cheese and ⅛ teaspoon reduced-sodium taco seasoning in a small bowl. Spread on the toast stars. Top with 1 tablespoon chopped tomato or green pepper.

PER SERVING: 85 calories, 3 g fat (2 g sat. fat), 8 mg chol., 197 mg sodium, 10 g carb., 2 g fiber, 4 g pro.

 X 1

GOLD NUGGET FRUIT POCKETS

These fruit-filled nuggets will cause a kitchen gold rush.

Ingredients

1   12-ounce package (10) refrigerated buttermilk biscuits

⅓ cup desired chopped, peeled fruit, such as apples, peaches, or pears

3   tablespoons sugar

½ teaspoon ground cinnamon

Tools

Measuring cups, measuring spoons, cutting board, sharp knife, resealable plastic sandwich bag, baking sheet, ruler, hot pads, wire cooling rack, wide metal spatula

MOVE IT!
Strengthen the muscles needed for digging by helping out in the garden or shoveling sand.

Let's Make It!

1 Turn on the oven to 350°F. Open biscuit can. Separate biscuits and place on the dry cutting board. Using the palms of your clean hands, flatten each biscuit to a circle about 3 inches in diameter. Place about 2 teaspoons of your desired fruit in the center of each flattened biscuit. Fold edges of each biscuit together and seal with your fingers. Gently form each biscuit into a ball.

2 Put sugar and cinnamon into the sandwich bag. Put 2 biscuits in the bag. Seal bag and shake until each biscuit is covered with the sugar-cinnamon mixture. Remove biscuits from bag and place on the baking sheet. Repeat to coat the remaining 8 biscuits, putting 2 in the bag at a time. Place balls 2 inches apart on baking sheet.

3 Bake about 12 minutes or until golden brown. Turn off oven. Use hot pads to remove baking sheet from the oven. Put baking sheet on the wire rack. Let biscuits cool completely. Use the spatula to remove the biscuits from the baking sheet.

PER SERVING: 126 cal., 5 g fat (1 g sat. fat), 0 mg chol., 340 mg sodium, 19 g carb., 0 g fiber, 2 g pro.

 X2

CRAZY PET MUFFINS

MAKES: 14 servings

Take a walk on the wild side with these kooky creatures.

Ingredients

Nonstick cooking spray
½ cup golden raisins
Hot water
2 cups all-purpose flour
⅓ cup toasted wheat germ
1½ teaspoons baking powder
½ teaspoon baking soda
½ teaspoon salt
½ teaspoon ground cinnamon
1 egg, lightly beaten
1¼ cups buttermilk
½ cup packed brown sugar
¼ cup vegetable oil
1 cup shredded carrots
1 recipe Cream Cheese Spread
1½ to 2 cups shredded wheat cereal
   or bite-size corn square cereal,
   coarsely broken into shreds, or
   1 cup shredded coconut, toasted
28 marshmallows and/or banana slices
28 whole almonds and/or semisweet
   chocolate pieces
Raisins and/or dried apricots
14 dried apricots and/or fresh
   blueberries

Tools

Measuring cups, measuring spoons, shredder, muffin pans with fourteen 2½-inch muffin cups, paper bake cups, 3 small bowls, medium bowl, spoon, colander, wooden toothpick, hot pads, wire cooling rack, small resealable plastic bag, scissors, table knife

Let's Make It!

1 Turn on the oven to 400°F. Put a paper bake cup in each of the muffin cups. Lightly coat paper bake cups with cooking spray. Set aside. Put golden raisins in a small bowl. Pour enough hot water over raisins to cover. Set aside.

2 Put flour, wheat germ, baking powder, baking soda, salt, and cinnamon in the medium bowl. Use the spoon to make a sunken place in the center of the flour mixture.

3 Put the egg, buttermilk, brown sugar, and oil in another small bowl; mix well. Pour the egg mixture into the flour mixture. Stir until moist (batter will be lumpy). Drain the raisins. Add raisins and carrots to the batter, gently stir until mixed.

4 Spoon batter into the prepared muffin cups, filling each cup about three-fourths full. Bake for 18 to 20 minutes or until golden brown and a toothpick stuck near the center comes out clean. Turn off oven. Use hot pads to remove pans from oven. Put pans on wire racks. Cool for 5 minutes. Carefully lift muffins from muffin cups. Cool completely on wire racks.

5 To serve, place a small amount of the Cream Cheese Spread in the plastic bag. Seal bag. Use the scissors to snip off a small corner of the bag. Set bag aside. Spread the remaining Cream Cheese Spread evenly over muffins. Carefully sprinkle about 1 tablespoon of the cereal or coconut over the top of each muffin. Place 2 of the marshmallows or banana slices on the upper part of each muffin for eyes, squeezing out a little of the Cream Cheese Spread in bag to hold the marshmallows in place. Place 1 almond or chocolate piece in the lower portion of each eye. For a mouth, press a few raisins into the bottom center section of each muffin. (Or for a tongue, press a dried apricot into the bottom center section.) Place a dried apricot or blueberry in the middle of each muffin for a nose. Serve immediately or store in an airtight container in the refrigerator up to 3 days.

PER MUFFIN: 295 cal., 9 g fat (2 g sat. fat), 23 mg chol., 257 mg sodium, 50 g carb., 2 g fiber, 6 g pro.

 X1

Cream Cheese Spread: In a small bowl combine 6 ounces softened reduced-fat cream cheese (Neufchâtel) and 2 tablespoons honey. Stir until smooth.

MAGICAL DESSERTS

Get your wand (er, wooden spoon) and spells (ahem, recipes) ready! Follow along to transform basic ingredients into delicious desserts so good they'll vanish before your eyes. Abracadabra!

MAGIC CUPCAKES

Here's a magic trick everyone will eat up. A peanut butter cup placed on top of the batter of each cupcake disappears while baking—ta-da!

Ingredients

- 1 cup all-purpose flour
- ½ cup unsweetened cocoa powder
- ⅓ cup granulated sugar
- ⅓ cup packed brown sugar
- ½ teaspoon baking soda
- ¼ teaspoon baking powder
- ¼ teaspoon salt
- 2 egg whites
- ¾ cup fat-free milk
- ¼ cup canola oil
- 1 teaspoon vanilla
- 12 bite-size chocolate-covered peanut butter cups
- 1 recipe Peanut Butter Frosting

Tools

Measuring cups, measuring spoons, paper bake cups, muffin pan with twelve 2½-inch cups, medium bowl, spoon, large bowl, wire whisk, hot pads, wire cooling rack, fork, small saucepan, wooden spoon, table knife

Let's Make It!

1 Turn on the oven to 350°F. Put a paper bake cup in each of the muffin cups. Set aside.

2 Put flour, cocoa powder, granulated sugar, brown sugar, baking soda, baking powder, and salt in the medium bowl. Stir to mix.

3 Put the egg whites in the large bowl and whisk until mixed. Add milk, oil, and vanilla to the egg whites. Whisk to mix well. Add the flour mixture to the milk mixture. Whisk until smooth.

4 Using a ¼ cup measuring cup, scoop batter into prepared muffin cups. Fill each cup about half full. Set a peanut butter cup on the center of the batter in each cup.

5 Bake for 14 to 16 minutes or until tops spring back when lightly touched with your finger. Turn off oven. Use hot pads to remove pan from oven. Put pan on the wire rack. Cool cupcakes for 5 minutes. Carefully lift the cupcakes from muffin cups. Cool completely on wire rack.

6 Once cupcakes are cool, spread each with Peanut Butter Frosting. Serve once frosted or store in a single layer in an airtight container at room temperature for up to 3 days.

Peanut Butter Frosting: Put ¼ cup chunky peanut butter and 3 tablespoons butter in the small saucepan. Put on burner. Turn burner to low heat. Cook until melted. Stir all the time with the wooden spoon. Remove from heat. Add 1½ cups powdered sugar and 1½ teaspoons vanilla. Stir to mix well. Stir in 4 teaspoons milk. If frosting is too stiff to spread, stir in a little more milk to make spreading consistency. Makes about ¾ cup.

PER CUPCAKE: 299 cal., 13 g fat (4 g sat. fat), 8 mg chol., 197 mg sodium, 43 g carb., 2 g fiber, 5 g pro.

X ½   X 1

FAIRY FLOWER PUFFS

Made with light-as-a-fairy puff pastry, these sweets give your meal a fairy tale ending.

Ingredients

½ of a 17.3-ounce package (1 sheet) frozen puff pastry, thawed following package directions

All-purpose flour

2 kiwifruits, peeled and cut into small pieces

½ of a mango, peeled, seeded, and cut into small pieces

24 fresh raspberries

¼ of an 8-ounce container frozen fat-free whipped dessert topping, thawed

Tools

Measuring cups, cutting board, sharp knife, parchment paper, large baking sheet, 2½-inch flower-shape cookie cutter, hot pads, 2 wire cooling racks, pancake turner

Let's Make It!

1 Turn on the oven to 375°F. Line the baking sheet with parchment paper. Set aside.

2 Unfold puff pastry sheet and put it on a lightly floured surface. Dip the flower-shape cookie cutter into flour. Using the cutter, cut 12 flower shapes from pastry. Place pastry flowers on the prepared baking sheet.

3 Bake for 10 to 12 minutes or until puffed and golden. Turn off oven. Use hot pads to remove baking sheet from oven. Place baking sheet on a wire rack. Use the pancake turner to transfer pastries to another wire rack; cool completely.

4 To serve, carefully pull off the top half of each pastry; set tops aside. Place bottom halves on a wire rack. Spoon dessert topping onto bottom halves of each pastry. Arrange fruit pieces on top of dessert topping on pastries. Place pastry tops on fruit to make sandwiches. Serve right away or store unfilled puffs in an airtight container in the refrigerator for up to 3 days or the freezer for up to 1 month.

PER SANDWICH: 140 cal., 8 g fat (2 g sat. fat), 0 mg chol., 54 mg sodium, 16 g carb., 1 g fiber, 2 g pro.

X ½

MINI ELF COOKIES

Fresh from your kitchen workshop, these cookies are so delicious people will think you had magical helpers.

Ingredients

¼ cup butter, softened and cut up

¼ cup shortening or vegetable oil

½ cup packed brown sugar

¼ cup granulated sugar

¼ teaspoon baking soda

¼ teaspoon salt

1 egg

½ teaspoon vanilla

1½ cups all-purpose flour

½ cup miniature semisweet chocolate pieces

½ cup snipped dried cherries and/or pitted dried plums (prunes)

Tools

Measuring cups, measuring spoons, table knife, kitchen scissors, large mixing bowl, electric mixer, rubber spatula, wooden spoon, large cookie sheet(s), ruler, hot pads, pancake turner, wire cooling racks

Let's Make It!

1 Turn on the oven to 375°F. Put butter and shortening in the large bowl. Beat with the electric mixer on medium speed about 30 seconds or until butter is smooth. Add brown sugar, granulated sugar, baking soda, and salt. Beat on medium speed until combined, stopping the mixer a few times to scrape the bowl with the rubber spatula.

2 Add egg and vanilla. Beat on medium speed until combined. Add flour. Beat on low to medium speed until combined. Add chocolate pieces and dried fruit. Stir until combined.

3 Using a 1 teaspoon measuring spoon, scoop a rounded spoonful of dough and drop onto ungreased cookie sheet. Scoop additional dough mounds onto cookie sheet, leaving 1 inch between dough mounds.

4 Bake about 9 minutes or until edges of cookies begin to brown. Use hot pads to remove cookie sheet from oven. Use the pancake turner to transfer cookies to wire rack. Repeat with remaining dough, letting cookie sheet cool between batches. Turn off oven. Store leftover cookies in an airtight container, using waxed paper, if needed, to divide layers for up to 3 days or freeze for up to 1 month.

PER 2 COOKIES: 58 cal., 2 g fat (1 g sat. fat), 6 mg chol., 25 mg sodium, 8 g carb., 0 g fiber, 1 g pro.

 X ½

MOVE IT!
Go for a nature walk with
your parents to explore
an enchanted forest
(or your neighborhood).

JEWELED UNICORN HORNS

These enchanted treats are so fun they're mythical.

MAKES: 12 (1-horn) servings

Ingredients

- 1 10-ounce package marshmallows
- ¼ cup almond butter or peanut butter
- 2 tablespoons butter
- 6 cups whole grain crispy rice cereal
- ½ cup dried cranberries
  Butter, softened
- 3 ounces white baking chocolate or semisweet chocolate
- 1 teaspoon shortening
  Assorted colored decorating sugars or edible glitter

Tools

Measuring cups, measuring spoons, large saucepan, wooden spoon, hot pads, waxed paper, large cookie sheet, small microwave-safe bowl, spoon, 1-quart resealable plastic bag, scissors

Let's Make It!

1 Put the marshmallows, almond butter, and the 2 tablespoons butter in the large saucepan. Put saucepan on burner. Turn burner to medium-low heat. Cook until mixture is melted and smooth, stirring all the time with the wooden spoon. Turn off burner. Use hot pads to remove saucepan from burner. Add the cereal and the cranberries to the marshmallow mixture in the pan. Quickly stir with the wooden spoon until well mixed. Cool the mixture about 5 minutes or until cool enough to touch with your hands.

2 Put a piece of waxed paper on the cookie sheet. Rub a small amount of butter on your palms and fingers. Divide the cereal mixture into 12 equal portions (½ to ⅔ cup each). Use your hands to shape each portion into a cone about 6 inches tall. If you would rather make 24 smaller cones, use 24 equal portions (¼ to ⅓ cup each) and shape them into 3-inch-tall cones. Put each cone on the waxed paper on the cookie sheet.

3 Put the chocolate and shortening in the microwave-safe bowl. Microwave on 50 percent power (medium) for 1 minute. Stir chocolate. Microwave on 50 percent power (medium) for 30 seconds; stir again. Repeat until chocolate is melted and smooth.

4 Pour melted chocolate into the plastic bag. Seal bag. Use the scissors to snip off a small corner of the bag. Squeezing the bag, drizzle the chocolate in a spiral around the outside of each of the cereal cones. Quickly sprinkle with decorating sugar or edible glitter. Let the cones stand until the chocolate is set. Store leftover horns in an airtight container at room temperature for up to 3 days.

PER HORN: 253 cal., 9 g fat (4 g sat. fat), 9 mg chol., 161 mg sodium, 42 g carb., 1 g fiber, 3 g pro.

 X ½   X ½

RAINBOW FRUIT PIZZA

MAKES: 16 servings

At the end of this rainbow you're likely to find a line of people waiting to taste it.

Ingredients

- ⅔ cup butter, softened
- ¾ cup sugar
- 1 teaspoon baking powder
- ¼ teaspoon salt
- 1 egg
- 1 tablespoon milk
- 1 teaspoon vanilla
- 2 cups all-purpose flour
- ½ of an 8-ounce package reduced-fat cream cheese (Neufchâtel), softened
- 1 8-ounce container frozen fat-free whipped dessert topping, thawed
- 8 fresh strawberries, tops cut off and each berry cut in half
- 1 11-ounce can mandarin orange sections, drained
- 1 small fresh mango, peeled, seeded, and cut into small pieces
- 2 kiwifruits, peeled, sliced, and each slice cut into fourths
- ½ cup fresh blueberries
- ½ cup red seedless grapes, each cut in half

Tools

Measuring cups, measuring spoons, cutting board, sharp knife, can opener, colander, mango corer (if you like), large mixing bowl, electric mixer, rubber spatulas, parchment paper, large cookie sheet, pencil, ruler, plastic wrap, hot pads, wire cooling rack, medium mixing bowl, spoon, offset spatula

Let's Make It!

1 Put the butter in the large bowl. Beat with the electric mixer on medium speed about 30 seconds or until light and fluffy. Add sugar, baking powder, and salt to butter. Beat with the electric mixer on medium speed until well mixed, stopping the mixer a few times to scrape the bowl with a rubber spatula. Add egg, milk, and vanilla. Beat on medium speed until mixed. Add flour. Beat on low speed until mixed.

2 Put a sheet of parchment paper on the cookie sheet. Draw the shape of a rainbow on the parchment paper, making it 12 inches tall in the center and 5½ inches wide, and leaving a 5½-inch gap between the two ends of the rainbow. Press and shape the dough onto the rainbow shape (the dough should be about ¼ inch thick on the rainbow shape). Cover with plastic wrap and chill in the refrigerator for 30 minutes.

3 Turn on the oven to 375°F. Bake about 15 minutes or until edges are light brown and center is set. Turn off oven. Use hot pads to remove cookie sheet from oven. Set cookie sheet on wire rack and cool completely.

4 Wash the mixer beaters. Dry well. Put the cream cheese in the medium bowl. Beat with the electric mixer on medium speed until smooth. Add about half of the whipped topping to the cream cheese. Stir gently until mixed. Use a rubber spatula to gently fold in the remaining whipped topping. Use the offset spatula to spread cream cheese mixture over the cooled cookie crust (you may not use all the mixture).

5 Arrange strawberry halves, cut sides down, along the top edge of the cookie crust. Arrange orange sections under the strawberries. Arrange mango pieces under the orange sections. Arrange kiwifruit pieces under the mango pieces. Arrange blueberries under the kiwifruit pieces. Arrange grape halves, cut sides down, under the blueberries. Cut into 16 pieces. Store leftovers in an airtight container in the refrigerator for up to 3 days.

PER SERVING: 278 cal., 10 g fat (6 g sat. fat), 39 mg chol., 164 mg sodium, 42 g carb., 1 g fiber, 3 g pro.

 X1   X½

103

WIZARDING WANDS

Ingredients

6   ounces angel food cake, cut into 1-inch pieces (4 cups pieces)

1   8-ounce package reduced-fat cream cheese (Neufchâtel), softened

11   small raspberries, each cut in half, or 6 small fresh strawberries, tops cut off and each berry cut into fourths

8   ounces white baking chocolate and/or semisweet chocolate

4   teaspoons shortening

¼   cup graham cracker crumbs

Tools

Measuring cups, measuring spoons, cutting board, serrated knife, shallow baking pan, hot pads, wire cooling rack, wooden spoon, large resealable plastic bag, rolling pin, medium bowl, large bowl, waxed paper, 2 large baking sheets, small cookie scoop, 22 round paper lollipop sticks, small saucepan, heat-resistant rubber spatula

Work your culinary magic to create charming cake wands. When you're done casting spells, finish with a disappearing trick—eat the wand!

Let's Make It!

1 Turn on the oven to 300°F. Put the cake cubes in the shallow baking pan and spread to an even layer. Bake for 15 minutes. Use the hot pads to remove pan from oven and set on the wire rack. Stir the cake cubes. Bake for 10 to 15 minutes more or until cake cubes are golden brown and crispy. Turn off oven. Use the hot pads to take the pan out of the oven. Put the pan on the wire rack. Cool completely.

2 Put half of the cake cubes in the plastic bag. Seal bag. Using the rolling pin, roll over the cubes in the bag until they are finely crushed. Pour the cake crumbs into the medium bowl. Use the plastic bag and rolling pin to crush the remaining cake cubes. Pour into the bowl with the other cake crumbs. You should have about 1 cup cake crumbs.

3 Put cream cheese in the large bowl. Stir until smooth. Add cake crumbs to the bowl with the cream cheese. Stir to mix well.

4 Put a piece of waxed paper on each of the baking sheets. Scoop a 1-inch mound of the mixture into your opposite hand. Use your finger to make a dent in the ball. Put a piece of raspberry or strawberry into the dent. Shape the cream cheese mixture around the raspberry or strawberry. Roll the mound into a ball. Put the ball onto 1 of the prepared baking sheets. Repeat with the remaining cream cheese mixture and berries. Put the baking sheets in the freezer and freeze for 30 minutes. Push a lollipop stick into the center of each ball, pushing it almost to the other side. Freeze 30 to 60 minutes more or until balls are firm.

5 Put chocolate and shortening in the small saucepan. Put pan on burner. Turn burner to medium-low heat. Cook until chocolate is melted and smooth, stirring every now and again with the rubber spatula. Use the hot pads to remove the pan from the heat. Working in batches, dip the balls into melted chocolate. Allow excess to drip off and place balls on the clean waxed paper-lined baking sheet. Before chocolate sets, immediately sprinkle tops of balls with graham cracker crumbs. Let stand until chocolate is set. Store leftover wands in an airtight container in the refrigerator for up to 3 days.

PER WAND: 117 cal., 7 g fat (4 g sat. fat), 9 mg chol., 112 mg sodium, 12 g carb., 0 g fiber, 2 g pro.

X ½

MOVE IT!
Gather friends to play magic tag. When you tag someone, cast a spell on her to act out (for instance, melt like an ice cube or act like a monkey).

MAGIC POTION SHAKES

Add the secret ingredients to your whirling countertop cauldron—um, blender—to concoct a spellbinding fruity elixir.

Ingredients

3   cups frozen mango chunks

⅔   cup orange juice

½   pint (1 cup) raspberry sorbet

2   tablespoons fat-free milk

Tools

Measuring cups, measuring spoons, blender, 4-cup glass measure, rubber scraper, four 5- to 6-ounce glasses

Let's Make It!

1 Put mango and orange juice in the blender. Cover blender with the lid. Blend on high speed until smooth. Pour mango mixture into the glass measure. Use a rubber scraper to get all the drink out of the blender. Rinse the blender with water and shake out any excess water.

2 Put raspberry sorbet and milk into the blender. Cover blender with the lid. Blend on high speed until smooth.

3 Pour some of the raspberry mixture into each glass; carefully pour some of the mango mixture into each glass to form layers.

PER SERVING: 155 cal., 1 g fat (0 g sat. fat), 0 mg chol., 5 mg sodium, 38 g carb., 3 g fiber, 2 g pro.

 X1

Drinkable Chocolate Covered Strawberries: Put 1½ cups frozen unsweetened strawberries in the blender. Let berries stand in the blender at room temperature about 20 minutes or until slightly thawed. Add 2 tablespoons milk. Cover blender with the lid and blend on high speed until almost smooth. If necessary, turn off blender and push berries toward blade with a rubber scraper. Turn off blender. Add 1½ cups light vanilla ice cream to the blender with the strawberries. Cover blender with the lid and blend on high speed until smooth. Turn off blender; set aside. Put ⅛ cup hot fudge ice cream topping in a microwave-safe bowl. Put bowl in microwave. Set the microwave to cook for 30 seconds on 50 percent power (medium). Start microwave. Use hot pads to remove bowl from microwave. Stir sauce using a spoon. Set the four 5- to 6-ounce glasses on the counter. Use the spoon to drizzle half of the warmed chocolate sauce around the insides of the glasses (use about 2 teaspoons chocolate in each glass). Pour the strawberry drink into the glasses, filling each glass about three-fourths full. Use the rubber scraper to get all the drink out of the blender. Drizzle the tops of the drinks with the remaining chocolate sauce.

PER SERVING: 207 cal., 6 g fat (3 g sat. fat), 16 mg chol., 113 mg sodium, 35 g carb., 2 g fiber, 4 g pro.

X½

KNOW IT!
The mango is the most widely eaten fruit in the world!

PARTY TIME

Break out the decorations and noisemakers and gather your friends. It's time to celebrate! Your pals will have a dog-gone good time devouring these yummy party eats.

CONFETTI CRUNCH MIX

The explosion of colors and flavors in this munch mix will be the bright spot of any party—rain or shine.

Ingredients

- 2 cups pretzel nuggets
- 2 cups fruit-flavor round whole grain cereal
- ¼ cup whole almonds or peanuts
- 3 tablespoons honey
- ½ teaspoon ground cinnamon
- ½ cup yogurt-covered raisins
- ¼ cup dried cranberries
- 2 ounces white baking chocolate, chopped

Tools

Measuring cups, measuring spoons, cutting board, sharp knife, 15x10x1-inch baking pan, parchment paper, large bowl, small bowl, spoon, large rubber spatula, hot pads, wire cooling rack, small microwave-safe bowl, small rubber spatula, small resealable plastic bag, large airtight storage container

Let's Make It!

1. Turn on the oven to 350°F. Line the baking pan with parchment paper.

2. Put pretzels, cereal, and almonds in the large bowl. Put honey and cinnamon in the small bowl. Stir to mix. Drizzle the honey mixture over the pretzel mixture. Using the rubber spatula, stir until all the ingredients are coated with honey. Scrape mixture into prepared baking pan and spread into an even layer. Bake for 3 minutes. Using rubber spatula and hot pads, stir mixture.

Bake for 3 minutes more. Stir again. Bake about 4 minutes more or until toasted. (You will bake the mixture for 10 minutes total.) Turn off oven.

3 Use hot pads to remove pan from oven. Put pan on the wire rack. Cool for 10 minutes. Spoon mixture into serving bowl. Sprinkle raisins and cranberries over mixture. Stir to mix well.

4 Put white chocolate into the microwave-safe bowl. Microwave on 50 percent power (medium) for 1 minute. Stir chocolate. Microwave for 10 seconds more; stir again. Repeat until chocolate is melted and smooth. Scrape melted white chocolate into the plastic bag. Seal bag. Use scissors to snip off a very small corner of the bag.

5 Squeezing bag, gently drizzle chocolate over mixture in serving bowl. Let cool completely until chocolate is set. Serve right away or store in an airtight container at room temperature for up to 3 days. Makes 6 cups.

PER SERVING: 155 cal., 4 g fat (2 g sat. fat), 1 mg chol., 119 mg sodium, 27 g carb., 1 g fiber, 3 g pro.

 X ½

FRUIT FIZZIES

Whip up a fruity whirlpool in your blender, pour, and serve. Guests will dive right in.

Ingredients

- 8 large fresh strawberries, stems cut off and each berry cut in half
- 3 cups chopped, seeded watermelon
- 2 cups cool water
- ¼ cup sugar
- 1 tablespoon lime juice
  Ice, if you like
- 1 1-liter bottle sparkling water, chilled
  Fresh strawberries and/or small watermelon wedges, if you like

Tools

Measuring cups, measuring spoons, cutting board, sharp knife, citrus juicer, blender, fine-mesh sieve, large bowl, rubber spatula, large metal spoon, pitcher, 8 to 10 small glasses

Let's Make It!

1 Put the halved strawberries, the chopped watermelon, the water, and sugar in the blender. Cover blender with lid. Blend on high speed about 1 minute or until mixture is smooth and sugar is dissolved. Put the sieve over the large bowl. Pour fruit mixture into sieve, using the rubber spatula to scrape down sides. Using the back of the metal spoon, press lightly on blended fruit. Let stand about 15 minutes or until liquid has drained out of blended fruit. Pour liquid into a pitcher. Throw away fruit left in sieve.

2 Stir lime juice into liquid in pitcher. Put pitcher in refrigerator about 1 hour or until chilled.

3 When ready to serve, fill each glass about two-thirds full with the juice mixture. If you like, add a little ice to each glass. Fill each glass with sparkling water. If you like, add a strawberry and/or a watermelon wedge to each glass.

PER SERVING: 46 cal., 0 g fat, 0 mg chol., 2 mg sodium, 12 g carb., 0 g fiber, 0 g pro.

X ½

KNOW IT!
Because watermelons are 92% water, early explorers carried them as canteens.

HOLIDAY CELEBRATION CUPCAKES

Dress up these cupcakes for any special occasion using your favorite fruits and candies.

Ingredients

- ½ cup pitted dried plums (prunes), chopped
- ½ cup hot water
- 1½ cups all-purpose flour
- ¾ cup sugar
- ½ cup unsweetened cocoa powder
- ½ teaspoon baking soda
- ¼ teaspoon baking powder
- ¼ teaspoon salt
- 1 egg
- 1 egg yolk
- ¼ cup canola oil
- ½ teaspoon vanilla
- ⅓ cup buttermilk
- ¼ cup miniature semisweet chocolate pieces
- 1 recipe Frosting

  Assorted fresh berries, cut-up fruit, candies, and/or cookie crumbs

Tools

Measuring cups, measuring spoons, cutting board, sharp knife, muffin pan with twelve 2½-inch muffin cups, paper bake cups, small bowl, food processor, medium bowl, rubber spatulas, large mixing bowl, electric mixer, wooden spoon, wooden toothpick, hot pads, wire cooling rack, medium mixing bowl, table knife or small metal spatula

Let's Make It!

1 Turn on the oven to 350°F. Put a paper bake cup in each of the muffin cups in the muffin pan.

2 Put chopped plums in the small bowl and add the hot water. Let stand for 5 minutes. Pour mixture into the food processor. Cover and pulse with several on/off turns until plum mixture is smooth.

3 Put flour, sugar, cocoa powder, baking soda, baking powder, and salt in a medium bowl. Stir to mix well. Set aside.

4 Put the whole egg and the egg yolk into the large bowl. Beat with the electric mixer on high speed about 3 minutes or until slightly thick and lemon colored.

5 Add oil and vanilla to egg mixture. Beat with the electric mixer on medium speed about 2 minutes or until well mixed and smooth, stopping the mixer a few times to scrape the bowl with a rubber spatula. Stir in the plum mixture.

6 Add half of the buttermilk to the egg mixture. Stir to mix. Add half of the flour mixture. Stir to mix well. Stir in the last of the buttermilk. Stir in the last of the flour mixture. Stir in miniature chocolate pieces. Using a ¼ cup measuring cup as a scoop, scoop batter into muffin cups, filling each cup about three-fourths full.

7 Bake 20 minutes or until a toothpick stuck in the center of a cupcake comes out clean. Turn off oven. Use hot pads to remove pan from oven. Put pan on the wire rack. Let cupcakes cool.

8 Spread each cupcake with 2 to 3 teaspoons of the Frosting. Decorate as you like. Store leftover cupcakes in an airtight container in the refrigerator for up to 3 days.

Frosting: Put 6 ounces reduced-fat cream cheese (Neufchâtel), softened; 3 cups powdered sugar; and ½ teaspoon vanilla in a medium mixing bowl. Beat with the electric mixer on medium to high speed until smooth, stopping the mixer a few times to scrape the bowl with a rubber spatula.

PER CUPCAKE: 344 cal., 10 g fat (4 g sat. fat), 46 mg chol., 187 mg sodium, 60 g carb., 2 g fiber, 5 g pro.

X1

My PIES

Let your friends choose their favorite fruity flavor and these tiny pies will be a giant crowd-pleaser.

MAKES: 12 servings

Ingredients

1   15-ounce package (2 crusts) rolled refrigerated unbaked piecrust

Nonstick cooking spray

All-purpose flour

1   recipe Cinnamon Apple, Honey Peach, or Very Berry Fruit Filling

Tools

Muffin pan with twelve 2½-inch muffin cups, rolling pin, 4-inch cookie cutter, sharp knife, medium bowl, spoons, hot pads, wire cooling rack, small thin knife. If needed: vegetable peeler, cutting board, 15x10x1-inch baking pan, paper towels, small bowl

Let's Make It!

1 Turn on the oven to 375°F. Let piecrusts stand following package directions. Lightly coat each muffin cup with cooking spray.

2 Unroll 1 of the piecrusts onto a lightly floured work surface. Using the rolling pin, roll out crust to a circle that is 12 inches in diameter. Using the cookie cutter, cut 6 circles from crust.* Save scraps. Gently press each circle into a muffin cup. Repeat with the other piecrust. Using a sharp knife or pizza cutter, cut thin 2½-inch-long strips from the scraps of the 2 crusts.

3 Spoon your fruit filling choice into crust-lined muffin cups, spooning the same amount of fruit mixture into each muffin cup. Arrange about 6 of the piecrust strips in a crisscross design on each muffin cup. Throw away any extra piecrust strips.

4 Bake for 20 to 25 minutes or until crusts are browned and fruit is bubbling. Turn off oven. Use hot pads to remove pan from oven. Put pan on the wire rack. Let cool for 5 minutes. Run a small thin knife around the edge of each pie to loosen. Carefully remove pies from muffin cups. Serve warm or let stand until completely cooled. Store leftover pies in an airtight container in the refrigerator for up to 3 days.

*Tip: If you don't have a 4-inch round cookie cutter, use a 4-inch cup or can to mark circles in the piecrust. Use a knife to cut out the circles.

Cinnamon Apple Pie Filling: Using a vegetable peeler, carefully remove peel from 3 apples. On a cutting board use a sharp knife to cut apples into 4 pieces each. Cut out core and chop apple into ¼-inch pieces (you should have about 3 cups). In a medium bowl put apples, ⅓ cup packed brown sugar, and ½ teaspoon ground cinnamon. Using a wooden spoon, stir until combined.

PER PIE: 199 cal., 9 g fat (3 g sat. fat), 0 mg chol., 147 mg sodium, 29 g carb., 2 g fiber, 1 g pro.

 **X 1** **X ½**

Honey Peach Pie Filling: Line a 15x10x1-inch baking pan with 3 layers of paper towels. Put a 16-ounce package of frozen unsweetened peach slices on paper towels in a single layer. Let thaw for 30 minutes. On a cutting board, using a sharp knife, cut peaches into about ¼-inch pieces (you should have about 3 cups). In a medium bowl place peaches and 2 tablespoons honey. Using a wooden spoon, stir until combined.

PER PIE: 198 cal., 9 g fat (3 g sat. fat), 0 mg chol., 145 mg sodium, 28 g carb., 1 g fiber, 1 g pro.

 X 1

Very Berry Pie Filling: In a medium bowl put 3 cups cleaned raspberries, blueberries, blackberries, and/or chopped strawberries. In a small bowl put ½ cup sugar and 2 tablespoons cornstarch. Using a small spoon, stir until combined. Sprinkle sugar mixture over berries. Using a wooden spoon, gently stir until berries are coated with sugar.

PER PIE: 215 cal., 9 g fat (3 g sat. fat), 0 mg chol., 145 mg sodium, 32 g carb., 2 g fiber, 1 g pro.

X 1

MONSTER BASH PARFAITS

There's nothing scary about layers of cake, fruit, and ice cream. Parfaits are sure to be a monster hit!

Ingredients

- 2 to 3 slices purchased or leftover angel food cake, torn into bite-size pieces
- 16 fresh strawberries, tops cut off and berries cut into thin slices
- ⅓ cup strawberry spreadable fruit or strawberry jam
- 8 reduced-fat chocolate sandwich cookies with white filling
- 1 cup vanilla frozen yogurt
- ½ cup hot fudge ice cream topping, warmed
- 4 fresh strawberries, halved if you like

Tools

Measuring cups, cutting board, sharp knife, eight 10- to 12-ounce glasses, small bowl, spoon, small resealable plastic bag, coffee mug or rolling pin, plastic wrap, small ice cream scoop

Let's Make It!

1 Divide cake among the glasses. Put some of the sliced strawberries on top of the cake in each glass.

2 Put strawberry spreadable fruit or jam in the small bowl. Stir until smooth and spoon over strawberries in glasses.

3 Put cookies in the plastic bag. Seal bag. Using the coffee mug or rolling pin, roll over cookies until they are crushed a little bit.

Sprinkle crushed cookies over strawberries in glasses. Cover glasses with plastic wrap. Put in refrigerator until ready to serve (up to 5 hours).

4 When ready to serve, let frozen yogurt stand at room temperature for 10 minutes to soften. Scoop some of the frozen yogurt into each glass. Drizzle each with hot fudge topping. If you like, top each glass with a strawberry half.

PER PARFAIT: 231 cal., 5 g fat (2 g sat. fat), 16 mg chol., 163 mg sodium, 43 g carb., 1 g fiber, 5 g pro.

 X½   X½

PARTY PIZZAS

Every party needs pizza. With this personalized pie, guests can add their favorite toppings, bake, and eat.

MAKES: 12 (2-piece) servings

Ingredients

Nonstick cooking spray

4   6- to 8-inch whole wheat tortillas

6   tablespoons pizza sauce, taco sauce, or barbecue sauce

28   slices turkey pepperoni, 4 ounces shredded cooked chicken, or 4 ounces sliced cooked chicken sausage

¼   cup sliced pitted ripe olives, if you like

¼   cup chopped green or red sweet pepper, if you like

2   small chopped roma tomatoes, if you like

1   cup shredded mozzarella or Monterey Jack cheese (4 ounces)

Tools

Measuring cups, measuring spoons, cutting board, sharp knife (if needed), shredder, large baking sheet, small spoon, hot pads, wire cooling rack, pancake turner, pizza cutter

Let's Make It!

1 Turn on the oven to 400°F. Coat the baking sheet with cooking spray. Arrange tortillas on the prepared baking sheet. Spread sauce evenly on the tortillas. Arrange turkey pepperoni on top of the sauce. If you like, sprinkle with olives, sweet pepper, and/or tomatoes. Sprinkle cheese over toppings.

2 Bake for 8 to 10 minutes or until tortillas are beginning to brown around edges. Turn off oven. Use hot pads to remove baking sheet from oven. Put baking sheet on the wire rack. Cool for 5 minutes. Use the pancake turner to move 1 pizza at a time to the cutting board. Use the pizza cutter to cut each pizza into 6 pieces.

PER 2 PIECES: 66 cal., 4 g fat (2 g sat. fat), 14 mg chol., 202 mg sodium, 5 g carb., 3 g fiber, 5 g pro.

121

PUMPKIN BITES

It won't require any tricks to get friends to try these treats. Packed with pumpkin and drizzled with caramel, they're frightfully good.

MAKES: 24 (1-bite) servings

Ingredients

Nonstick cooking spray
1 cup all-purpose flour
½ cup whole wheat flour
½ cup quick-cooking rolled oats
¼ cup toffee pieces
1½ teaspoons baking powder
¼ teaspoon salt
¼ teaspoon pumpkin pie spice
1 egg, lightly beaten
¾ cup canned pumpkin
¼ cup packed brown sugar
¼ cup milk
3 tablespoons canola oil
3 tablespoons butterscotch-caramel ice cream topping

Tools

Measuring cups, measuring spoons, can opener, muffin pans with twenty-four 1¾-inch muffin cups, large bowl, medium bowl, spoons, small spoon or cookie scoop, wooden toothpick, hot pads, wire cooling rack, fork, serving platter, small resealable plastic bag, scissors

Let's Make It!

1 Turn on the oven to 350°F. Coat the muffin cups with cooking spray. Set aside.

2 Put all-purpose flour, whole wheat flour, oats, toffee pieces, baking powder, salt, and pumpkin pie spice in the large bowl. Stir to mix.

3 Put egg, pumpkin, brown sugar, milk, and oil in a medium bowl. Stir to mix well.

4 Add pumpkin mixture to flour mixture. Stir just until combined. (Batter will be thick.) Using a small spoon or cookie scoop, scoop batter into muffin cups, filling each cup nearly full.

5 Bake 14 minutes or until a toothpick stuck in the center of a muffin comes out clean. Turn off oven. Use hot pads to remove from oven. Put pan on the wire rack. Cool 5 minutes. Use the fork to remove muffins. Place muffins on the platter.

6 Put caramel topping into the plastic bag. Seal bag. Use scissors to snip off a small corner of the bag. Squeezing bag gently, drizzle caramel over muffins. Store undrizzled bites in an airtight container in the refrigerator for up to 3 days or the freezer for up to 1 month.

PER SERVING: 82 cal., 3 g fat (1 g sat. fat), 11 mg chol., 69 mg sodium, 13 g carb., 1 g fiber, 2 g pro.

X ½

MOVE IT!
Play your favorite Halloween music and dance like a monster, ghost, or zombie.

TEA PARTY FUN

Brew up some fun with bite-size sandwiches. Choose one flavor or all four. Whatever you decide, the perfect party is in the (tea) bag.

Strawberry Dessert Sandwiches

Using a serrated knife, cut 16 thin slices off a purchased loaf of pound cake. Using a table knife, spread 8 of the slices with 3 ounces softened reduced-fat cream cheese (about 2 teaspoons per slice). Top cream cheese with 3 tablespoons strawberry spreadable fruit (about 1 teaspoon per slice). Top with ½ cup thinly sliced strawberries. Top with remaining slices of pound cake. Press down gently on sandwiches. Using serrated knife, cut sandwiches into squares, strips, and/or triangles. Top each tea sandwich with a slice or wedge of strawberry, if you like. Makes 8 servings.

PER SANDWICH: 176 calories, 8 g fat (3 g sat. fat), 38 mg chol., 200 mg sodium, 25 g carb., 0 g fiber, 3 g pro.

 X ½

Bite-Size Ice Cream Sandwiches

Place 16 vanilla wafers in a 13x9x2-inch baking pan. Using a small cookie scoop, scoop 1 cup of vanilla ice cream onto wafers (about 1 tablespoon per cookie). If ice cream begins to melt, work with half of the cookies at a time. Cover with foil and put in freezer for 1 hour. Put 1 ounce chopped white baking chocolate in a small microwave-safe bowl. Microwave on 50 percent power for 10 to 15 seconds at a time until melted, stirring with a spoon each time. Scrape melted chocolate into a small resealable plastic bag. Cut a very small corner off bag. Do the same with 1 ounce of semisweet chocolate. To make tops for sandwiches, place 16 vanilla wafers on a baking sheet. Drizzle with chocolates and place in freezer until chocolate is firm. Place tops on ice cream sandwiches and return to freezer for 3 hours until firm. Makes 16 cookie sandwiches.

PER SANDWICH: 94 cal., 4 g fat (2 g sat. fat), 4 mg chol., 46 mg sodium, 13 g carb., 0 g fiber, 1 g pro.

B-L-Tea Sandwiches

Put 6 thin slices of firm whole wheat bread on a cutting board. Using a serrated knife, cut off crusts. In a small mixing bowl stir together ⅓ cup cooked and finely crumbled bacon with ¼ cup light sour cream. Spread mixture on 3 of the slices of bread. Top with 2 thinly sliced small plum tomatoes. Top tomatoes with ½ cup finely shredded lettuce. Top with the other 3 slices of bread. Using serrated knife, cut sandwiches into squares, strips, and/or triangles. Push toothpicks through small grape tomatoes and then into sandwiches. Makes 8 servings.

PER SANDWICH: 98 cal., 5 g fat (2 g sat. fat), 11 mg chol., 250 mg sodium, 10 g carb., 2 g fiber, 5 g pro.

 X1

Cucumber Hummus Tea Sandwiches

Spread ⅓ cup of your favorite purchased hummus on 16 whole grain crackers (about 1 teaspoon per cracker). Sprinkle with a little sweet paprika. Sprinkle ¼ cup of chopped, unpeeled seedless cucumber on each cracker. Using a clean hand, press cucumber into hummus lightly. Top each cracker with a little shredded carrot. Sprinkle with a little more paprika, if you like. Makes 8 servings.

PER SANDWICH: 31 cal., 2 g fat (0 g sat. fat), 6 mg chol., 32 mg sodium, 2 g carb., 0 g fiber, 2 g pro.

X ½   X ½

INDEX

METRIC INFORMATION

PRODUCT DIFFERENCES

Most of the ingredients called for in the recipes in this book are available in most countries. However, some are known by different names. Here are some common American ingredients and their possible counterparts:

- Sugar (white) is granulated, fine granulated, or castor sugar.

- Powdered sugar is icing sugar.

- All-purpose flour is enriched, bleached or unbleached white household flour. When self-rising flour is used in place of all-purpose flour in a recipe that calls for leavening, omit the leavening agent (baking soda or baking powder) and salt.

- Light-color corn syrup is golden syrup.

- Cornstarch is cornflour.

- Baking soda is bicarbonate of soda.

- Vanilla or vanilla extract is vanilla essence.

- Green, red, or yellow sweet peppers are capsicums or bell peppers.

- Golden raisins are sultanas.

VOLUME AND WEIGHT

The United States traditionally uses cup measures for liquid and solid ingredients. The chart (above right) shows the approximate imperial and metric equivalents. If you are accustomed to weighing solid ingredients, the following approximate equivalents will be helpful.

- 1 cup butter, castor sugar, or rice = 8 ounces = ½ pound = 250 grams

- 1 cup flour = 4 ounces = ¼ pound = 125 grams

- 1 cup icing sugar = 5 ounces = 150 grams

- Canadian and U.S. volume for a cup measure is 8 fluid ounces (237 ml), but the standard metric equivalent is 250 ml.

- 1 British imperial cup is 10 fluid ounces.

- In Australia, 1 tablespoon equals 20 ml, and there are 4 teaspoons in the Australian tablespoon.

- Spoon measures are used for smaller amounts of ingredients. Although the size of the tablespoon varies slightly in different countries, for practical purposes and for recipes in this book, a straight substitution is all that's necessary. Measurements made using cups or spoons always should be level unless stated otherwise.

COMMON WEIGHT RANGE REPLACEMENTS

Imperial / U.S.	Metric
½ ounce	15 g
1 ounce	25 g or 30 g
4 ounces (¼ pound)	115 g or 125 g
8 ounces (½ pound)	225 g or 250 g
16 ounces (1 pound)	450 g or 500 g
1¼ pounds	625 g
1½ pounds	750 g
2 pounds or 2¼ pounds	1,000 g or 1 Kg

OVEN TEMPERATURE EQUIVALENTS

Fahrenheit Setting	Celsius Setting	Gas Setting
300°F	150°C	Gas Mark 2 (very low)
325°F	160°C	Gas Mark 3 (low)
350°F	180°C	Gas Mark 4 (moderate)
375°F	190°C	Gas Mark 5 (moderate)
400°F	200°C	Gas Mark 6 (hot)
425°F	220°C	Gas Mark 7 (hot)
450°F	230°C	Gas Mark 8 (very hot)
475°F	240°C	Gas Mark 9 (very hot)
500°F	260°C	Gas Mark 10 (extremely hot)
Broil	Broil	Grill

*Electric and gas ovens may be calibrated using celsius. However, for an electric oven, increase celsius setting 10 to 20 degrees when cooking above 160°C. For convection or forced air ovens (gas or electric), lower the temperature setting 25°F/10°C when cooking at all heat levels.

BAKING PAN SIZES

Imperial / U.S.	Metric
9x1½-inch round cake pan	22- or 23x4-cm (1.5 L)
9x1½-inch pie plate	22- or 23x4-cm (1 L)
8x8x2-inch square cake pan	20x5-cm (2 L)
9x9x2-inch square cake pan	22- or 23x4.5-cm (2.5 L)
11x7x1½-inch baking pan	28x17x4-cm (2 L)
2-quart rectangular baking pan	30x19x4.5-cm (3 L)
13x9x2-inch baking pan	34x22x4.5-cm (3.5 L)
15x10x1-inch jelly roll pan	40x25x2-cm
9x5x3-inch loaf pan	23x13x8-cm (2 L)
2-quart casserole	2 L

U.S. / STANDARD METRIC EQUIVALENTS

⅛ teaspoon = 0.5 ml

¼ teaspoon = 1 ml

½ teaspoon = 2 ml

1 teaspoon = 5 ml

1 tablespoon = 15 ml

2 tablespoons = 25 ml

¼ cup = 2 fluid ounces = 50 ml

⅓ cup = 3 fluid ounces = 75 ml

½ cup = 4 fluid ounces = 125 ml

⅔ cup = 5 fluid ounces = 150 ml

¾ cup = 6 fluid ounces = 175 ml

1 cup = 8 fluid ounces = 250 ml

2 cups = 1 pint = 500 ml

1 quart = 1 litre